Trialogue
between Jew,
Christian and Muslim

THE LITTMAN LIBRARY OF JEWISH CIVILIZATION

EDITORS
David Goldstein
Louis Jacobs
Lionel Kochan

This Library is dedicated to
the memory of

JOSEPH AARON LITTMAN

Trialogue
between Jew,
Christian and Muslim

IGNAZ MAYBAUM

ROUTLEDGE & KEGAN PAUL   LONDON

First published in 1973
by Routledge &Kegan Paul Ltd
Broadway House, 68-74 Carter Lane,
London EC4V 5EL
Printed in Great Britain by
Alden & Mowbray Ltd
at the Alden Press, Oxford

ISBN 0 7100 7682 7

To the memory of
SIEGMUND MAYBAUM (1844-1919)
Rabbi and Teacher of Rabbis

Contents

Preface

I regard this book as a kind of commentary on Franz Rosenzweig's *The Star of Redemption* (1971), which is now available to English-speaking readers in a translation published by Routledge & Kegan Paul as a volume of the Littman Library of Jewish Civilization (editors: Louis Jacobs and David Goldstein). This is frequently referred to in the text as *Star*. I am sure that Franz Rosenzweig is for modern Jewry what Maimonides was for medieval Jewry. Maimonides called his philosophical treatise *Guide for the Perplexed*. With Franz Rosenzweig's *The Star of Redemption* contemporary Jewry has received its Guide for the Perplexed.

The trialogue between Jew, Christian and Muslim which is the subject of my book has often been dealt with by scholars who are experts in the field of comparative religion. I have not ignored the findings of these scholars. But as the author of this book I do not see myself as writing about facts of a past history. I write about events which have taken place and are hotly debated within contemporary Jewish history. The holocaust, the establishment of the State of Israel, the changes affecting the life of diaspora Jewry are the events in which I have observed the beginning of, and the necessity for, a trialogue between Jew, Christian and Muslim. This trialogue sometimes becomes articulate. But sometimes, although passionately experienced, it remains below the level of consciousness. I see it as my task to bring those involved in mute confrontation to the point where words can help towards an understanding of differing views. The westernized Jew argues with the help of doctrines, whereas the not yet westernized Jew relies on a legal framework, on the *halachah*, for his religious life. This antithesis between doctrine and Law has forced on the modern Jew a participation in the Christian-Islamic dialogue which with the Jewish response is widened into a trialogue.

The material of my book consists of papers which I read at the Leo Baeck College for the training of rabbis for the progressive sector of Jewry. I think of the students, who listened to me, argued with me and made suggestions, as co-workers, and as friends who afforded me decisive help.

They now serve in congregations in Anglo-Jewry, on the Continent, in Israel, in South Africa; in fact all over the world. When this book reaches them they will, I am sure, remember the creative hours we spent together. I want to say that I wrote this book thinking above all of the 'College family' of the Leo Baeck College.

I wish to make it clear that 'the historical Jesus' of the Unitarian is not the God of the New Testament and not the God of the Old Testament. The Unitarians have no contribution to make to the trialogue which Jews, Christians and Muslims can pursue and yet remain Jews, Christians and Muslims. The God of the Unitarian is the product of the syncretism prevalent in times of religious decline. It is the true Christian faith, the faith of the Christian Church, with which the Jew and Muslim can engage in a trialogue to find the common ground of the three monotheistic religions.

From the bottom of my heart I thank my wife, who typed the manuscript and performed the various technical tasks which go with the publication of a book. Without her this book would not have been written.

Next to her my thanks go to my dear pupil Dr Nicholas de Lange, Lecturer in Rabbinics in the University of Cambridge, who read the manuscript and freed it from German phraseology without changing my style. I am also grateful to him for his many comments and valuable suggestions.

Last, but not least, I wish to express my sincere thanks to Rabbi Dr David Goldstein.

Acknowledgments

I want to thank the following authors and publishers for permission to quote passages or sentences from books for which they have the copyrights:

Professor Nahum N. Glatzer, Brandeis University: *Franz Rosenzweig: His Life and Work*, The Jewish Publication Society of America; Mr George Steiner, Churchill College, Cambridge: *T.S. Eliot Memorial Lectures*, first published in the *Listener*, 8 April 1971, later in *Bluebeard's Castle*; Allen & Unwin: Ortega y Gasset, *The Revolt of the Masses*; Oxford University Press: Kenneth Cragg, *Alive to God*; Weidenfeld & Nicolson: Walter Laqueur, *Europe Since Hitler*; Edward Arnold: Johan Huizinga, *The Waning of the Middle Ages*; and Harper & Row: Johan Huizinga, *Men and Ideas*.

Last but not least I thank Routledge & Kegan Paul for the opportunity to quote the various passages from Franz Rosenzweig's *The Star of Redemption* published by them in the translation by William W. Hallo.

CHAPTER I

From Hasidism to Theology

THE WORD HASID BEFORE HASIDISM

The occurrence of the word Hasidim in Psalm 35, 'Sing praise unto the Lord, ye His Hasidim', and in similar texts of the *Tenach*, does not entitle us to speak of Hasidism in biblical times. Hasid as a biblical word denotes a man who worships God, a man who is pious. The eighteenth-century word Hasid means something else.

In the Book of the Maccabees the word Hasidim appears in its Greek version: *Assidaioi*. The Maccabees are the *Assidaioi* who fight against Antiochus for their religious autonomy.

After an interval of two centuries the term Hasidim reappears in the Mishnaic and Talmudic literature. Hanina ben Dosa and Honi the Circle-maker belong to a group called Hasidim. They differ from the rabbis of their period in the alleged success of their prayers. Their *Halachah* was more severe than the law of the rabbis. They were religious eccentrics, even experimenting with magic. Hanina ben Dosa 'proved' that the bite of a scorpion to which he exposed his heel would not kill him; his prayers would save him. Honi stood in the middle of a circle which he would not leave until his prayers were fulfilled. The Mishnaic term 'rabbis and Hasidim' implies a distinction: Hasidim, not rabbis. These Hasidim never established themselves as an organized party within the Jewish people, as did the Pharisees and Sadducees. The rabbis tolerated them, even with a limited amount of favour. The common people admired the 'miracles' which these men were believed to have performed (see S. Safrai, 1965).

In the Middle Ages the term Hasidim reappears again in the phrase 'The pious of Germany (*Hasidei Ashkenaz*) and the scholars of Spain'. These Hasidim in the Jewish communities in Germany lacked what the Sephardim had in great measure: Jewish learning, cultural refinement, prosperity and, up to 1492, security. Rabbi Yehuda ben Shemuel, called 'the pious' (*he-Hasid*), who lived in Worms and died in 1216, is one of these Hasidim. In the *Sefer ha-Hasidim* (The Book of the Pious) we become acquainted with the religious ideals of this rabbi and his followers, which were not so different from those of Christian monks. Whereas in eighteenth-century Eastern European Hasidism the Baal Shem aimed at joy in religious practice, the 'Pious of Germany', living in the age of the barbaric crusaders, made asceticism, though not sexual asceticism, their ideal. There is no connection between the *Hasidei Ashkenaz* and the Hasidic movement of the Baal Shem.

THE CHARISMATIC RABBI

Adolf von Harnack speaks of the twofold message of the Gospels. He points to the two different ways in which Jesus is referred to. He is seen as a messiah, or as a rabbi, a teacher. In this role he performs a function like many others before and after him in Jewish history. He is a man with a message. But there is also another Jesus in the text of the Gospels: Jesus, in whom the people believed. Belief in God changes into belief in Jesus, who appears as Christ, as the Anointed, as Lord. This belief makes Christianity a faith different from Judaism. About the sermons, parables, doctrines of Jesus (most of which, in any case, go back to Jewish sources, to the Torah) there could be a dialogue between Christians and Jews which need not make Christianity into a Jewish schism. The belief in Jesus as a person different from any human being was and is in Jewish eyes departure from Jewish mono-theism.

This irreconcilable contradiction – 'belief in the teachings of Jesus' against 'belief in Jesus himself' – recurs again and again in history whenever a leader is allowed to wield charismatic power. The charismatic teacher may appear to teach and preach like any teacher and preacher, but he is not a teacher or a preacher. He is a leader. The charismatic gift in a person may be necessary to make a good teacher or a successful political speaker. But the important point must not be left unnoticed. Teaching and preaching establish a personal relationship between teacher and taught, between preacher and religious flock. Charismatic teaching does not really teach but fascinates, and creates in this way a compact following of believers.

Charismatic teaching created the little groups which were made up of those Eastern European Jews who entered Jewish history as Hasidim. These Jews believed in their rabbis. Initially they were not rabbis, they were an uneducated clergy, often element-ary-school teachers, but their followers were even less educated in the teachings of Jewish tradition. The lame led the blind. But these lame leaders had the great ability to speak about religious matters in a way ordinary people understood. The recipients were grateful. Out of this gratitude rose a fervent belief: the belief in their rabbis. This belief itself changed the rabbis. They had to adjust themselves to the belief of their admiring flock. They became saints. They also became impostors and charlatans.

It is a well-known fact that Christian readers are attracted by the Hasidic literature which Buber brought to the literary market of the West. It seemed to give them an astounding but fitting commentary to the Gospel story. Here was a rabbi performing miracles; he attracted disciples as Christ did: the Gospel story all over again, repeated in the villages and hamlets of Eastern Europe.

To study, to learn, to read books is a high priority in Jewish religious life. But did the followers of the Hasidic rabbis really study? To a certain degree they did. A Jewish population in districts without rabbis profited from the sermons and inter-

3

pretations of the Hasidic rabbis. The humble beginnings of the Hasidic movement had merits which must not be forgotten in the face of the later decadence of Hasidism which soon set in. This decadence and depravation were inevitable, and resulted from the very nature of charismatic teaching. A proper student–teacher relationship maintains a sober, rational atmosphere. The charismatic teacher has an irrational hold on his pupil. He overwhelms the personality of those who enter his magic circle. A strong person assaults a weak one. This is the genesis of the belief in the charismatic person. Jewish life is Jewish through the predominant role of its teachers. The Hasidic rabbi as charismatic teacher arouses belief but does not teach. Here lies the un-Jewish root of Hasidism.

Leonardo da Vinci's painting of the Last Supper is known to every educated person. What we see in the painting moves us. The man in the centre of the twelve disciples is different from them. In him is a power which makes the twelve a unit. It is his charismatic power. As Jews we can understand this charismatic hold of one person on another, while refusing to be spellbound by the charismatic leader. In the painting *The Last Supper* only men take part in the solemn meal. So it is with the Hasidic meal. The rabbi at the head of the table is surrounded by men who follow him fascinated by his charisma. This creates a relationship which is un-Jewish, as it subordinates the recipient to the charismatic dispenser of whatever it may be: advice, guidance or promise of success or healing. The giver of these things is revered as a saint and the recipient is reduced to the role of the humble admirer and grateful believer. Where there is one person of high-ranking authority and others flocking around him in a mass, an un-Jewish community is established. Hasidism is a movement which, in spite of its early creative influence as Jewish Pietism, was bound to become the target of an opposition which defended true Judaism against heresy. The *Mitnaggdim*, as the opponents of Hasidism were called, represented true, unadulterated Judaism. Hasidism was eventually bound to lead to fundamentalism, superstition and a despicable form of business in which so-called rabbis exploited pious fools.

The true relationship between a rabbi and his followers becomes clear through the two Hebrew words *haver* (a disciple who follows the rabbi but is socially equal to him) and *talmid* (a pupil who has chosen a rabbi as his tutor). 'Ben Azai was the *haver* (disciple) and the *talmid* (pupil) of Rabbi Akiba' (j. Shek. III, 47b). *Haver* does not mean 'comrade'. It means a man who associates himself with a rabbi and learns from him. True Jewish life comes into existence where a rabbi, his wife and children establish a study community with others, their wives and children. The Hasidic gathering is not a gathering of families. Men leave their families and attend the male gathering around one who is charismatically gifted. What is a charismatic person? Only those who believe in one can answer. Those who are sane will never understand those who are mad. Of course, the Greeks spoke of 'holy madness'. Greeks and Jews represent the difference between gentile and Jew.

MARTIN BUBER AND HIS BIOGRAPHERS

Buber was twenty-seven years of age when he published his first two volumes of *Tales of the Hasidim*. At that time, 1905–6, he lived in Florence. The rich young man enjoyed a life of leisure, reading books, swimming and rowing and being a Romantic. Buber, who never missed anyone who counted in the world of literature, was reading R. M. Rilke, who in his lyric opus replaced religion by the worship of beauty. Searching for the pattern of a Jewish culture the young Buber, like Rilke, saw the poet in the role of the prophet. In Hasidism, as he saw it, Buber found Jews not shaped by Western rational bourgeois civilization but in a garb which a Romantic could relish: Jews outside their homes roaming the countryside from village to village, united not through 'dry' doctrine but through an inspired, ecstatic teacher. The small groups in their occasional gatherings were, to say the least, not part of the Establishment. This negative characteristic made them appear as the vanguard of a true, Romantic protest. So Buber saw it in Florence.

Buber, although born in Lemberg, was in the same position as every assimilated Western Jew, searching for and returning to Judaism. He did not bring any traditional knowledge of Judaism into his career as a Jewish writer. His parents were divorced, and he grew up in the house of his grandfather, who was a Jewish scholar shaped by the Enlightenment movement. Buber went to a Polish Grammar School, and at that time Polish was his language. He was a polonized Jew, when he went from Lemberg to Vienna. German was not his natural idiom. 'He writes German better than we do, or writes it worse, but he does not write German as we write it', said Stapel, a German critic of Buber's literary output. There is a reason for the difficulty of which many readers of his works complain. Buber is often difficult to understand. But the situation becomes worse in the English translations of Buber's works. The American authors Maurice Friedman, Malcolm L. Diamond and others who write about Buber sometimes write about a man who never existed. The vagueness of the German text gives the translator ample opportunity to add his own views in the name of Buber. There is no biography of Buber which gives a sober assessment of the life and work of the man. What we have are hagiographies, not biographies.

Of the Vienna which shaped Martin Buber's youth and, indeed, his whole life, the playwright Arthur Schnitzler said, 'We all play, and the man who knows this is wise.' At Vienna University Ernst Mach's agnosticism represented the ruling philosophy. Buber in his *Kultur-Zionismus* struggled to emancipate himself from this *fin de siècle* pessimism. His aestheticism could not be the right means to achieve this aim. But he was always ready to accept help when it was offered. Two men exerted decisive influence on him: Gustav Landauer (see p. 111) and Franz Rosenzweig.

In 1914 Franz Rosenzweig was invited by Buber to write an article for a yearbook. The article is now published in *Kleinere Schriften* (see Rosenzweig, E., 1937) with the title 'Atheistic Theology'. It was rejected by the editors of the yearbook, probably by Buber himself. However this may be, anyone who read the article in 1914 must have come to the conclusion 'Franz

Rosenzweig and Buber – never the two can meet'. It happened differently. The two collaborated for years, in fact until Rosenzweig's death, in a most creative friendship. For Buber it meant that he discovered the *Tenach*, the Hebrew Bible.

He did not turn away from Hasidism, in which he retained his interest, since the public continued to see him as the author who had unearthed a forgotten movement. But during his co-operation with Rosenzweig, who hardly referred to Hasidism either in his *Star* or in his later works, he made an important alteration in the second edition of his *Die chassidischen Bücher* ('Hasidic Books'; 1927): the word 'ecstatic' as attributed to Hasid was either crossed out or replaced by another word. But his whole concept of Hasidism remained unchanged. Buber often speaks of the doctrine of Hasidism and fails to see that there is none. He does not see that Hasidism is a liturgical movement which changed the service of the Sephardi synagogue into the different form of service of the Ashkenazi synagogue. To this important change Buber remained blind. This is not surprising: Buber was never a synagogue-goer. Those who did not read his learned essays and books and knew him as he lived among his fellow-Jews were convinced that he was an agnostic; true, a committed Zionist, but otherwise an un-Jewish Jew.

After Franz Rosenzweig's death in 1929 Buber finished their translation of the Bible by himself, but later he abandoned his biblical studies. He is again the Zionist writer, but as before in a peculiar way. He preaches humanism, the *Humanitäts-Ideal*, as the German expression goes, but makes humanism the means to propagate his branch of nationalism. Here he is assisted by his brand of German. He speaks of Zion, and makes all those who search for clarity in his use of the word 'Zion' despair. Zion – is it the concept of the prophets or is it the political slogan of Jewish nationalism? In all Buber's essays the question remains unanswered. He gives his answers in a form of German which is the profound language of the humanist philosopher and is also a form of German which is what the Germans call *Schwulst* (swollen, inflated, bombastic language). Of his work as a philosophical writer Buber said that it was often a walk on a high mountain ridge from which

7

there was no small danger of falling. So far Buber's confession. Indeed, those who move in the world of abstract thought or in the elated world of the preacher are exposed to danger: when the strength to uphold the tension fails, then they write *Schwulst*. In the vault of the Munich library I have seen the manuscripts of Schelling's *Die Weltalter*. On nearly every page whole sentences, sometimes whole paragraphs, were crossed out. Buber was a creative thinker, but his work would have benefited from a massive pruning.

In defence of Buber's occasional lapse into *Schwulst* it must be said that he accepted the German concept of *Kultur*, especially in his *Reden über das Judentum* (Lectures on Judaism), given to Jewish students in Prague and first published in 1911. This concept of *Kultur* is never clear, as it is a sociological term imbued with religious meaning. In the dark glimmer of German metaphysics *Kultur* is made to appear as transcending reality. Whoever does not use his reason is deceived. In his romantic period Buber was deceived. He soon grew out of this phase, but the two volumes of the *Reden* have not been withdrawn. They are still in circulation and quoted, with approval.

After I had written this chapter, I read Walter Kaufmann's *I and Thou* (1970). With the suggestion that Buber was deliberately obscure, Kaufmann certainly goes too far. He writes: 'Obscurity is fascinating' (p. 19), and adds the strange statement: 'A lack of clarity is almost indispensable to the survival of a book' (p. 20).

Buber as a Zionist writer is master of the art of being misunderstood. One type of reader approves of the Zionist Buber and is made to ignore the humanist liberal in him. The other type respects the humanist liberal in Buber and does not recognize the crude nationalism, strongly inherent but hidden in Buber's lectures and essays. Thus Buber as a propagandist enjoys the best of two worlds: he is a liberal to the liberals and a Jewish nationalist to the Zionists. A similar ambivalence arises in Buber's description of the Hasidim. They recommend themselves to the liberal Western Jew as religious groups, and to the Zionists as a movement which, like any national movement, brings 'people' (*Volk*), not 'merely' individuals, on to the stage of history.

Buber was an eclectic writer. He was a different person at different times. In 1933 Rabbi Baeck asked me: *'Was lehrt er jetzt?'* (What does he teach now?) We made out a list of authors – Jewish and non-Jewish – who had at some time been Buber's authorities. Buber had a fine ear for what was in vogue and this is often the secret of his success. But many who write about Buber telescope these various stages of his development into one single position, and the result is – especially with his American admirers – the biography of a man who never existed. In 1933, when Baeck put the above-mentioned question to me, Buber was not yet world-famous. The German rabbis – liberal and orthodox – rejected the man who was to them a romantic youth leader, dispensing German romanticism in a Jewish cloak.

Buber is always the champion of prophetic biblical universalism, forceful, convincing and most sincere. He is constantly preaching the cause of mankind, critical of national particularism. But by a kind of linguistic alchemy he subtly avoids being involved in the antithesis of 'universalism versus particularism'. During the twenties these two terms became in the West the slogans which, like battle cries, differentiated synagogue from synagogue, one set of preaching rabbis from another. Buber had his followers in both camps. He was an honest man. But owing to his form of German, which was moulded by German metaphysics and at the same time prone to *Schwulst*, his 'double think' remained hidden to his admirers and above all to himself. He was a Zionist, but he let his Zion appear as a spiritual city in which all liberals – shaped by an unrealistic dream about mankind – would one day feel at home. His success up to 1933 was that of a leader who commanded the following of romantic Jewish youth. After 1933 the 'dialogue' stopped and emigration to Palestine became flight. This does not mean that Buber was right and the liberals wrong. It meant that in Hitler's Europe a world catastrophe had trampled down liberalism. To the question, 'Negation or affirmation of the diaspora?' we have a statement from Buber, for him unusually straightforward. In 1918 Buber writes to Stefan Zweig:

Today only this remark, that I know nothing of a 'Jewish State

9

with guns, flags and medals', not even in the shape of a dream. . . .
In any case I prefer participating in the enormous, daring experiment
of something new, in which I do not see a lot of 'good living' but
a great series of sacrifices, to enduring life in a diaspora any longer
(Hans Kohn, 1961, p. 170).

Eventually the universalist theme recedes and in his last-but-one
book, written in 1950, *Israel and Palestine*, Buber (1952) arrives at
what can be called a 'blood and soil' ideology. Three years later
he published *Eclipse of God* (Buber, 1953), with which he won a
grateful audience among the Atlantic community. I must repeat
my earlier warning against telescoping the various forms in
which Buber appears in his writing into one man with the name
of Buber. This 'one Buber' is fiction. Buber, the man who lived
among us, is a man in whom irreconcilable contradictions
existed side by side, or, to put it in a different way, who wrote
books and essays so different from each other that they might
have been written by different authors.

In 1952 Buber received the Goethe Prize, in 1954 the Peace
Prize of the German book trade, in 1960 the Annual Cultural
Award of the City of Munich. The Municipality of Tel Aviv
honoured him with the Bialik Prize in 1961. Shortly before
Buber's death, the Mayor of Jerusalem rushed into the home of
the sage to tell him that he had received the Freedom of the city
of Jerusalem.

Buber deserved the gratitude expressed in these honours. His
brand of Zionism brought many Western Jews to Palestine and,
later, to Israel, who would not have heeded the mere call of
nationalism. Buber insisted that the way back to Israel was a
'holy way'. This is the title of a little book which made a deep
impression on the young Jews and Jewesses who said farewell
to Europe and began a new life in the kibbutz.

All the honour and publicity accorded to Buber by his contemporaries and by posterity had one side-effect. It became a
wall behind which a man greater than Buber was hidden from
view: Franz Rosenzweig. A satisfactory biography has not yet
been written. It would show that everything that was thought,
felt and tried out in Buber's time is chronicled and discussed in

his writings. All trends of thought in this era were investigated, to find out whether they could contribute to the salvation of the Jewish people and of mankind. Buber is the great, perhaps the greatest Jewish personality of the years before and after the holocaust. Rosenzweig leads into the future in which we shall have to live.

Buber's Hasidism has to be judged from a point of view which sees prophetic Judaism, the Judaism of the *Tenach*, as the standard by which we accept or reject any movement which in the course of history assumes the attribute 'Jewish'. Buber's Hasidism is a deviation from prophetic Judaism. Today, Hasidism has become a Jewish drop-out movement. Early Hasidism made an important contribution to Eastern European Jewish life, which lacked synagogues and places of Jewish education such as the *Heder* and *Yeshivah*. It soon became a distorted, even decadent branch of Judaism.

Buber longed all his life for what he called *Gemeinschaft*, which means 'fellowship', and aims at union with fellow-man and fellow-Jew. To him this German word *Gemeinschaft* had a numinous quality. He lowered his voice to a devotional whisper when he pronounced it. He was uprooted from his Polish, German and even from his Jewish origins. He never understood and never participated in that fellowship through which the synagogue unites its worshippers: close human brotherliness through communal prayer, and at the same time a freedom which prevents the stifling embrace of collectivism. As he was a Jew, not at home in the synagogue, Buber hoped to get from Hasidism what other Jews receive from the synagogue. In this he was mistaken.

Buber was a prolific writer. He did not write because he knew; he wrote because he wanted to know. By writing he expressed himself. But writing, above all, was the means for his research. Although he advocated dialogical thinking, in his life the written, not the spoken, word was the mighty force by which he could reach out and find his fellow-man. Buber worked on himself like a sculptor on a marble bust. The orator standing on a platform has to adjust himself to his public. Buber watched the impression he made. The reason need not have been vanity, but a shyness which all public figures feel more or less. Buber continually chiselled away at himself, until he became to an admiring crowd the charismatic teacher he imagined the Hasidic rabbi to be.

What of Buber's vast work will endure beyond our time? What he wrote between 1933 and 1939 in Germany under the very noses of the Gestapo belongs to the literature of resistance. It brought hope, it taught dignity and was gratefully read not only by Jews but also by Christian theologians, and it had its echoes in many a sermon preached by ministers belonging to the Confessional Church. These essays were published in Germany by Schocken up to 1938. An English translation was brought out by the same publishers in New York (see Buber, 1948). After 1945 Buber reached a wide English-speaking public. His *Paths in Utopia* (1949) must be read as Buber's *Apologia pro vita sua*. The old sage did not recant what he wrote as a preacher of the Zionist or socialist millennium. But the attentive reader of *Paths in Utopia* will hear a man different from the one who addressed the Prague circle in his youth. A resolute editor is needed for his biblical works *Königtum Gottes* and *Moses*. Buber included notes which were superfluous to the messages of prophetic religion, which became his main interest once he had fallen under Rosenzweig's influence.

HASIDISM AS PART OF EUROPEAN PIETISM

The initial mistake when assessing Hasidism is to isolate it from seventeenth- and eighteenth-century religious movements in Western and Central Europe. P. J. Spener (1635–1705), A. H. Francke (1693–1727), Count L. Zinzendorf (1700–60), John Wesley (1703–91) and the Bohemian Brethren are to Christian Pietism what the Baal Shem (1700–60) is to Hasidism. Christian Europe, after the Thirty Years' War, and Polish Jewry, after the breakdown of the three-*Kahal* system, lacked authoritative leadership. Old-established leaders faced the opposition of the new 'post-war' generation who had grown up without guidance.

Jews, dispersed over the countryside, had no communities to lean upon. There was a dearth of rabbis, teachers were scarce. The Jew from these isolated provinces, which had no seats of Jewish learning, became an *Am-Haarets*. According to an old tradition (see Hertz (ed.) 1947, 'Sayings of the Fathers', 2: 6) the *Am-Haarets*, the ignoramus, cannot be a Hasid, he is unable to be pious. Hasidism changed this statement from a negative to a positive meaning: the *Am-Haarets* is chosen; he is the very man capable of profound piety. Hasidism had its programme for the illiterate Jew.

A German historian of Pietism writes: 'The first centre of Pietism was the Cambridge of the sixteenth century' (Heppe, 1879). Testimony to the English origin of Pietism is the phrase 'the practice of piety'. The heart and soul of religious life is not the dogma or the law, entrusted to the care of a learned clergy, but piety practised by the praying worshippers themselves. *Praxis pietatis* versus theology! This is the new teaching of Pietism everywhere. The practice of piety is in the hands of all, even of ordinary people. Everyone, not only the theologians and the lawyers of the established religion, is included in the idea of a kingdom of priests. Spener is the first to interpret the kingdom of God as a kingdom of priests, the priests not being ecclesiastical officials, but lay priests. This interpretation meant the end of the feudal society and ushered in the democratic era.

Among the forerunners of Pietism were the Dutch 'Brethren of the Common Life'. They were monks living in monasteries. Their movement, which also had followers in Germany, was called *devotio moderna*. Indeed, the *devotio moderna* heralded a post-medieval religious life in the midst of the Middle Ages. These people, whom we can only classify as monks, said of themselves: '*Non sumus religiosi, sed in saeculo religiose vivere nitimur et volumus*' (We are not monks, but to live piously in the world is our aim). Looking back to monasteries of this kind in the Middle Ages, to these *fratres communis vitae* in Holland and Germany, Luther referred to them approvingly: 'Such monasteries and Houses of Brotherhood are to my liking.' Later they all joined the Reformation.

Jean Gerson, Chancellor of the University of Paris (1363–1429), defended the *devotio moderna* against the charge of Protestant heresy long before Luther. But while he was prepared to tolerate it in the Netherlands, he did not wish it to spread to his own country, France. The *devotio moderna*, like Pietism afterwards, was not to be found in Latin countries where Roman Catholicism remained in force. With its rich host of images, visible in sculpture and paintings, and with its numerous saints, Latin Christianity satisfies the imagination of the illiterate. Religious symbols have been called the books of the illiterate. The Lutheran reformation was fought at the universities; the professors of theology wrote their learned treatises and pamphlets, and ordinary people could not follow. Pietism reached the common man by appealing to 'inwardness'; Roman Catholicism satisfied his eye with a spiritual world made visible.

The character of a people is formed by its religion. The *devotio moderna* and Pietism shaped the German type of Christian, who was different from the Italian Christian. To change the scenery: the Lithuanian Jew, whom the Gaon of Vilna succeeded in keeping away from Hasidism, is different from, say, a Polish Jew. The Lithuanian Jew is well known as a rationalist type. Whether as a scholar or as a businessman, the *Litvak* displays clear thinking, whereas the Polish Jew is an emotional type, who, when westernized, has artistic gifts.

The man who 'practises piety' is *froom*, he has *godzaligheit*. These two words, which have their roots in Middle High German, indicate the entry of Pietism, located by the historian Heppe first in Cambridge, into the German realm. The man with a piety of a more peaceful nature is *froom*; the man with a piety of a more ecstatic nature has *godzaligheit*. The ascent from *froom* to *godzaligheit* is the ascent – to use the Hebrew terms – from *kavanah* to *hitlahavut*. The inwardness of *kavanah* is the source; no rivers can flow, unless they have their origin in this quiet but inexhaustible source. *Hitlahavut*, on the other hand, is an ecstatic, momentary experience, it is a bright spark. It may light up the darkness for a solitary moment, or cause a sad conflagration in the soul of the zealot. But both *kavanah* and *hitlahavut*, unreservedly exalted by Buber, must be assessed soberly and critically.

Hitlahavut is an intensive, but momentary experience. It is the religious fervour and passion of the dervish and the biblical prophet. Elijah, himself full of religious zeal, rejects the validity of ecstasy in itself (I Kgs. 19:11, 12). The best modern example of the momentary element of ecstatic experience is provided by John Wesley: on 24 May 1738, at 8.45 a.m. in the Community Home, Aldersgate Street, London, Wesley had the experience which showed him that 'the way to holiness is the *sudden* gift of faith'. Wesley organized his followers in a 'Holy Club'. So did the hasidic rabbi; his pious followers gathered in his 'court'. Yet, there is one phrase in the Jewish Prayer Book, well known to every Jew: 'Our God and God of our fathers'. When did our faith in God begin? Our faith is 'the faith of the fathers'. Passionate fervour is evident in the faith of the newcomer. Christians, for instance, are newcomers compared with Jews. Christian faith has a beginning, a turning-point, a sudden vision on the road to Damascus. True, each new generation consists of newcomers. But unless the newcomers perpetuate their youth in a youth movement, they realize, when they grow up, that what they regarded as new in their passionate first encounter, their 'conversion', is very old indeed. Before 1933 Buber's followers in Germany were first and foremost in the Jewish Youth Movement, in which German Romanticism was a strong, intoxicating ingredient.

Kavanah is also a passionate fervour, but without the momentary explosion of *hitlahavut*; it is, on the contrary, a continuous heat, like introvert passion. It is Kant's *gute Gesinnung* (good motive). All her life Kant's mother belonged to a Christian group who were devout Pietists. Kant himself is the philosopher of the French Revolution. He respected the Pietism of his mother but he did so as an outsider. The majestic words from his ethical treatise are: 'There is nothing to think of anywhere in the world that can without restriction be considered as good, except only good motive.' With these words Kant is still the true son of his mother. They can be quoted to explain the greatness of the German nation, but also provide an explanation of why the German nation brought disaster and destruction over Europe. If it is always the motive and not the deed itself, everything can at one time or another become 'good'. With such an approach duty is morally justified by its motive and not by its content. Thus millions obeyed Hitler; they did their duty. All this also has its bearing on the assessment of *kavanah* and *hitlahavut*. The fervour of being *froom* and of having *godzaligheit*, so piously experienced by Kant's mother, must not unreservedly be introduced into moral action, as was done by Kant. Full moral responsibility forces human conscience to weigh soberly whether an action deserves absolute support or utter rejection. Piety, too, must not exclude intellectual consideration.

The moral irresponsibility of Kant's ethics of good intention, of exclusively stressing the good motive, lies in the absence of any indication of the ethical content. Mere emphasis on *kavanah*, on devotion in prayer, with neglect of the content of prayer, can also lead to irresponsibility in regard to doctrine. The following Hasidic story of how a small boy's whistling proved more efficacious than all the prayers of a large congregation is the pattern which exalts *kavanah* and *hitlahavut* and overlooks their limitations:

A farmer who used to pray every year on the high holydays in the synagogue of the Baal Shem had a son who could neither read nor write. After the boy reached his thirteenth birthday, his father took him to synagogue on the Day of Atonement. The sacredness of the day filled the boy's heart as he stood in the midst of the congregation. Unable to follow their prayers, he wanted to express himself in some way. From his pocket he took a small whistle which he used while tending the cattle in the field, and he blew the whistle with all his might. The members of the congregation were terrified and perplexed, but the Baal Shem said: 'God has opened the gates of grace. The wrath of the Lord is averted. Every desire to serve God which comes from a pure and simple soul is sufficient and perfect in the eyes of the Lord.'

This story is typical of the Hasidic approach and is repeated again and again in similar forms. Whether the prayer comes from classical Judaism, such as the *Oleinu*, the *Kaddish* or the *Amidah*, or whether it is the prayer of an illiterate Hasid or even a silly boy, does not matter. What matters is devotion: *Kavanah* and *hitlahavut* alone count. Heine knew better; he said: 'Jews pray theology.' Our prayer book is, indeed, a treasure house of Jewish doctrine.

Man who is *froom*, who has *godzaligheit*, need not have any knowledge of the doctrinal side of his faith. He may even have contempt for the scholars, who are the experts in doctrine and law. He has nothing to do with the learned volumes of the scholars; he has his devotional literature. All this can be said of Christian Pietism and Hasidism alike. Wesley's 'Holy Club' and the Hasidic circle meeting for the Third Sabbath Meal are principally of the same character. The following quotation from J. G. Weiss (1957) describes the situation at a Third Sabbath Meal:

> There is one distinct facet of the religious life of the circle which was subsequently to hold a position of central importance in the Hasidic Movement, and that is the place and function of the Third Sabbath Meal, the *Se'udah Shelishit* . . . The most striking feature of the meal as described here is that it is not taken in the family circle, but participation in it is meant to render the meal a social occasion. It takes place in the house of Rabbi Moshe, who is the head of the Rabbinical Court of Kutov. The participants of this afternoon meal stay at the table long into the night. The time is devoted to discussions on religious matters. There is no light but a numinous darkness surrounds the table, though there would have been a perfectly good halachic way of lighting candles after nightfall. It seems that the participants preferred to intensify the atmosphere by staying in darkness. This is keenly felt by a vulgar outsider, the butcher of the town, who is eager for the early termination of the meal, which had already been too prolonged for both his religious taste and material interests. He is anxious that the ritual slaughterer of the town, who is participating in the meal, should leave the table and get down to work. In order to bring the *Se'udah* to an early conclusion, the butcher bursts into the room with a candle in his hand, thus dispelling the numinous darkness and thus abruptly terminating the meal, a well calculated act, for which he died in excommunication.

There is a striking similarity between the romantic meetings by candlelight of the German Youth Movement and the Hasidic Third Meal gathering. Perhaps we should not think of the bearded Hasidim only as old men. To reach old age in the primitive life of Eastern Europe, with its lack of proper medical care, was obviously exceptional. The Hasidim were continually on the move; they were often on the road to visit a Hasidic rabbi, to bring messages and consult each other, without the aid of modern postal services. Young people like this sort of life on the roads. They walk off what they cannot think out. The Christian contemporaries of the Hasidim were certainly a youth movement; the theological faculty and the city clergy of Leipzig complain about the 'nuisance' which the followers of A. H. Francke were. They revolted against philosophy and against the established syllabuses of the academic courses, and, of course, against the casuistry of canon law. It was a revolt of the students against the professors. In Eastern Europe this revolt was carried out by the young teachers of the *Heder* (religion school for young children) against the Talmudists. In both camps, in the West and in the East, devotional literature was in demand, and scholarship was frowned upon. In Germany puritanical books of edifying and penitential content were translated from English into German, and in East European Hasidism mysticism was appreciated. But the mysticism which reached Eastern Europe no longer had the originality and power of medieval Islamic and Christian mysticism. Only fragments of the old mystical systems penetrated into Hasidism. The mysticism which satisfied the inquiring intellect in the Middle Ages now served to kindle the emotions of the Hasidim, their inwardness, their quest for true worship.

No literary documents exist which would prove the close connection between European Christian Pietism and Hasidism. This connection was achieved through people wandering on foot from West to East and from East to West. There were large numbers of these people. They were artisans, pedlars, people who could carry all their belongings with them. They were also refugees fleeing from religious persecution like the Moravian Brethren. The cities were closed, but the roads were free for people wandering to and fro. Thus the ideas of Pietism spread over a wide area, from Bohemia to John Wesley's England, from Holland to the far-off place in the East, where the Baal Shem's

Hasidism created a new form of Jewish worship.

We are tempted to compare the Baal Shem with Count Zinzendorf, because both were born in the same year (1700) and both died in the same year (1760). Are there other similarities connecting the two? We have no biographical details to rely on in the case of the Baal Shem, but we do have them in the case of Count Zinzendorf. There is a feminine streak in Zinzendorf. His education, when he was a child, was mostly in the hands of women. No paternal influence formed him. As a youth, almost a child still, he began to form 'religious friendships'. When grown up, he completed what he had begun in his early years. His pietistic village in Herrenhut was a kibbutz. When an institution, rather than parents, is responsible for the upbringing of children, a matriarchal society is bound to follow. The men and women of Herrenhut, who regarded their daily work as a sideshow and made religious practice their overriding concern, had a father-figure in Count Zinzendorf. They were all one family. That means, that the individual families were not families, shaped by a real father and by a real mother; they were governed by one 'father' only: by the Count or, to change over to the Hasidic scenery, by the rabbi, not revered as a master of learning, but followed as a saint. The feminine feature of Hasidism should not be overlooked. It is there where the individual Hasid is bound by admiration to his Hasidic rabbi. The stories praising the guidance of the Hasidic rabbi, and indeed the 'miracles' he was alleged to have performed, are adulations of a feminine type.

Hasidism did achieve a great success. When we emphasize religious doctrines – as we must – we are in danger of over-stressing mere intellectual discussion, in which the humanist too can share. When we are obedient to a law, we may become legalists. The one great question is: 'Can we pray?' Hasidism, in making prayer the issue, led away from soulless legalism and from *pilpul* – the intellectual acrobatics of scholasticism.

HASIDIC TUNES AND JEWISH PRAYER

Hasidism changed the way in which Jews prayed in the synagogue. The predominance of chanting disappeared from the synagogue, and prayers were sung in individual tunes and melodies. The service of the Sephardic synagogue came to an end in Eastern Europe. Islamic medieval religious civilization, with its chanting of the Koran and of the prayers, ceased to influence Jews at prayer, and was replaced by Christian influence. For sixteen hundred years Jewry had lived side by side with Christendom, but it was in Hasidism that Jews were influenced for the first time by an element of Christian civilization. And what a strong element it was! No art is nearer to the heart of the Christian than music. The material used in sculpture is stone, in painting canvas. Music is without any restrictive and limiting material and recommends itself as the art of the Protestant age, of the age of *sola fide*, of a spirituality soaring away from reality. Have Bach, Mozart, Beethoven nothing to do with Christianity? Who can doubt that they have? When Asians enjoy Beethoven's Ninth Symphony with understanding, missionaries will have little left to do.

The service of a modern Sephardic synagogue has no longer, or at least not sufficiently, preserved the service of the synagogue in which, say, Maimonides prayed in Spain or in North Africa. In the original Sephardic synagogue, situated in the midst of Islamic civilization, chanting created group worship: Forget what you are as an individual, rest peacefully in the worshipping congregation! The chanted prayer, the litany, is typical of the Middle Ages, but is of as lasting importance as the Middle Ages themselves. The great era of Gothic Christianity will remain a power in our own Western civilization.

Chanting in worship uses the praying individual as a messenger in order to bring the Holy Scripture from the past to the future and to ignore the waste land of the present; *tagveed*, correct reading of the text, is the Islamic command. The messenger, chanting his text, may not be conscious of what he carries from the past, blessed as it is with the nearness of God; yet he preserves the message and hands it on to a future generation.

The spiritual experience of hearing the portion of the Law chanted gives us some idea of the great splendour, and of the atmosphere of holiness, which the chanting of prayers once bestowed on our services. The criticism 'mumbling of prayers' may be justified, but points only to the decadence of what was once powerful piety. It also reveals a Protestant evaluation on the part of the critics. This Protestant criticism has its reason. A Western scholar once approached an Indian sage who chanted his holy text by heart. The Westerner wanted to discuss a particular verse of these texts: the sage alleged that he had never heard of this verse. After long explanations the verse was recognized as part of the text chanted by him all his life. Chanting preserves tradition, but no consciousness is added to the submission of the worshipper.

The chanted prayer, the litany, can be compared to the arabesque, in which the Mohammedan avoids disobedience to the Second Commandment. Art, as a mediator between God and man, is forbidden. Only the arabesque is allowed; the eye of the Mohammedan is not lured away from the One God. In the litany it is the ear which is safeguarded against the same apostasy. But in both cases the apostasy from monotheism into aesthetic religion is made impossible through the more technical device of using in the one case the arabesque, in the other the litany; in both cases no conscious choice has been made between monotheistic realism and aesthetic illusion. The clash between the two worlds has been avoided, not fought out. But today art, the urge to create, powerfully fascinates modern Promethean man, and the obedience to the Second Commandment has to be achieved in full consciousness, as it was in the days of the prophets. In our technological age creative man triumphs. He is tempted to by-pass the One Creator.

The Reformation demanded an awakening to personal religious consciousness. The chanting of prayers, like the Gothic windows which prevented the daylight from penetrating the house of prayer, became less appreciated. Now the people, and not only priests, monks and nuns, sang in the churches. The Eastern Church rejects the organ; the human voice should be heard.

The litany brought into the mosque-like buildings of the Sephardic synagogues a ceremony as stiff and as strict as the

C

ceremony of a Spanish Court or of a Roman Catholic Church. The litany, the chanting of prayers, was an effective means of preserving not only the exact words of the prayers but also their doctrinal content. Hasidism replaced chanting by melody, by the so-called 'Hasidic tunes'. It was an innovation. The German Reform movement accepted the liturgical reform of Hasidism. Whereas Eastern European Jews sang the texts from their prayer books to melancholic, Slavic tunes, German Jews had the synagogue music of men like Lewandowski and Sulzer. The compositions of these men are often watered-down Mendelssohn or Haydn, yet they warmed the hearts of the praying German Jew. Both German and Eastern European Jews borrowed from the surrounding culture. Why should the Hebrew prayer sung to a Russian folk-tune be more Jewish than Lewandowski's *Kedushah*, which still touches the hearts of Jewish refugees from Germany? The late Rev. Hermann Mayerowitsch once performed a programme of Jewish music on the B.B.C. Three days before his planned recital, B.B.C. listeners could hear the choir of the Don Cossacks. Our cantor of the London United Synagogue had to change part of his programme at the last moment; examples of the 'Jewish' music, which he had intended to sing, were sung by the Don Cossacks as Russian music. The Hasidic tunes are as Jewish as is Marc Chagall, who displays in his paintings a tradition to which the Russian ikon-painters strictly adhered.

A story often told in Hasidic circles is – as usual – about a miracle: The Baal Shem heard a gentile shepherd boy sing – or whistle – a lovely melody – and offered to buy the tune from him. The boy agreed, and the Baal Shem introduced this newly acquired tune when he led his followers in prayer. But from the very moment when the Baal Shem sung his prayer in this new way, the young gentile could no longer remember the tune which he had sung so often in former days. It was now only sung by praying Jews – a fitting commentary on the Jewish originality of Hasidic tunes.

Neither the Hasidic tunes, nor the Moorish style in which Jews in the Victorian era liked to build their houses of worship, should be called Jewish. No culture is ever specifically Jewish, no matter how much we Jews may have come to love it and to assimilate it to our own life. Our 'The Lord is One' of the 'Hear, O Israel' robs every culture of its absoluteness. If an architect were to rebuild the model of the Herodian Temple which every Jew regarded as his holy sanctuary, what would we see? Before our disillusioned eyes there would stand a Hellenistic building as glorious in its architecture as any of those temples which are the great monuments of Greek culture in the Mediterranean orbit, built for the worship of Athene, Zeus and other pagan gods. The Greek polis was a 'Temple-State'.

Hermann Cohen said of Spinoza: 'Cold as a Sephardi'. This hostile remark is, of course, absolutely wrong about Spinoza in particular and about Sephardic Jewry in general, but it reveals something about Cohen himself. With this remark Cohen stands before us as the German Jew, who, like the Eastern European Hasid, desires that warmth in religious life, which is a characteristic of any form of Pietism. 'Give me a Russian Chazan', was the longing outcry of many a warden of a synagogue in Germany; there, too, Jews went to synagogue 'to hear a good chazan'. Sephardic Jewry never experienced Pietism, which is a peculiarity of Ashkenazic Jewry, both in Eastern Europe and in Germany. Sephardic Jewry had mysticism, not Pietism, as a counter-balance to the decline of Judaism into a petrified legalistic religion. The word chazan means 'cantor' only in Ashkenazic Jewry. In Sephardic Jewry the chazan was an official whose duties extended further than those of an Ashkenazi chazan.

The controversy concerning the organ made it appear as if German Jewry and Eastern European Jewry were different in their forms of synagogue service. But it is a mistake to assume that the organ has created a new situation in the liturgical movement of post-medieval Jewry. The performance of a chazan, ambitious to display his artistic qualities, and an overdose of organ music, can both rob the synagogue of its sobriety. Ezekiel warns us against both attempts to provide a religious atmosphere through the aesthetic medium: 'And, lo, thou art unto them as a love song of one that hath a pleasant voice and can play well on

23

an instrument; so they hear Thy words, but they do them not'
(33:32). This prophet said his passionate 'no', when asked by
his fellow-exiles whether they should build a temple in Babylon.
The argument 'there was music in the Temple' overlooks the
fact that the synagogue must never be what the Temple was.
The Church, in the splendid use of art for her service, regards
herself as the successor of the Temple. The synagogue is what it is
because it led away from the Temple.

It is irrelevant whether the warmth which Eastern European
and German Jews introduced into the service was created by an
organ, a cantor or a choir. All the arguments against the organ
have nothing to do with the controversy which divides Reform
and Orthodox Jews. The only existing forum in the Anglo-
Jewish community where ministers of Reform and of Orthodox
synagogues meet as members of one group is the 'Union of
Anglo-Jewish Preachers'. I once lectured at a meeting of this
organization, which still survives from the happier, more tolerant
days of Anglo-Jewry. My subject was 'The Organ in the Jewish
Service'. I read aloud the following passage from a book:
'Orthodoxy does not use musical instruments. There is no
organ . . . as substitute for the human voice, for the praises
chanted by man; musical sounds without words, without
meaning, although musically beautiful, tend to make the service
worldly.' I asked my colleagues who they thought the author
was. Somebody guessed, 'the late Chief Rabbi Dr Hertz';
another, 'Solomon Schechter'. I closed the book, and they could
read its author and title: Sergius Bulgakov, *The Orthodox Church*.

The organ, the Slavic tunes of Eastern European Hasidism,
synagogue music imitated from Felix Mendelssohn, they all
equally enriched our divine services and also brought us near to
the danger of slipping away from Jewish prayer into aesthetic
fascination. This danger is absent in a synagogue which has no
chazan. The absence of the chazan, in itself not yet a significant
fact, had important consequences. The reading of prayers made
the spoken word the characteristic of a new Jewish divine service.
An innovation was made, different from the innovation which
Hasidism introduced into the chanted service of the Sephardic

tradition. We Jews are told, in the Second Commandment, not to take aesthetic values for religious values. The mistake is avoided – although not always – in the service in which anglicized Jews pray without a chazan. Admittedly, this service, too, can through its choir become like a concert, dispensing aesthetic uplift, but the absence of a chazan makes the reading of prayers a new feature of the service and restores the spoken word to its proper importance, which chanting and singing had often diminished.

When we read a prayer, we cannot evade its true purpose. When we pray, we pray to God. Have we the courage to do so? Have we the strength to do so? If we have not that courage and that strength, and that trust from which courage and strength grow, help is available: The prayer can be sung or chanted. The prayer sung in a sweet melody brings us to God with the help of art, which acts as a mediator between ourselves and God. Yet a Jew should not have a mediator. The prayer chanted in solemn, dignified monotony brings us to God by placing us before Him not as individual worshippers but as members of a worshipping group. Here again a warning is due. We should pray as individual persons and not hidden in the group. When we read a prayer, read it ourselves, not helped by anything or anybody, then we really pray.

I am told that the warmth of the service disappears when prayers are only read and neither chanted nor sung. In answer to that I have three points to make. First of all, as I have already admitted, a proper balance of chanting, reading and singing is required; my plea is only for recognition of the new contribution which the service without a chazan has made. Second, the so-called warmth of the service can often be the happy distraction from what is otherwise too difficult: it is sometimes, perhaps always, difficult to pray. Finally the absence of warmth in the service can be nothing else than the price which has to be paid for raising into the consciousness of the spoken word what otherwise remains below the level of consciousness. This price is no sacrifice. It buys something essential: the true Jewish atmosphere. The Jewish atmosphere is sober and of prosaic nature. Prose is the attribute of reality, and reality is created by God (see Maybaum, 1960, pp. 48–70).

It is the old argument against the synagogue: the connoisseur of the mystery cults of antiquity and the Christian who despises the aesthetic poverty of the *Judenschule*, both miss what the synagogue does not intend to provide – the enthusiastic uplift, which can be experienced by a newcomer. The Christian walks as it were on tiptoes in his church; the Jew is at home in the synagogue. When Archbishop Fisher went on his tour for the sake of union among the Churches, he met a dignitary of the Greek Orthodox Church. This gentleman forgot that the Church of England is a Protestant Church, and expressed his disapproval of the Roman Catholic Church as the 'first Protestant Church', saying of her liturgy: 'as cold as a Methodist Church'. Those who point to the 'lack of warmth' in a Liberal or a Reform synagogue should consider whether they do not complain of something which is, in fact, essential in a synagogue.

In emphasizing the importance of reading the prayers, I do not refer to the controversy over whether our Hebrew prayers should be read in the vernacular. A hundred years ago the early Reform movement was involved in this controversy: today the problem is settled. An entirely new situation has arisen: Hebrew has become the vernacular of a part of the Jewish people. Prayer, in Hebrew or in the vernacular of the diaspora, must arise from the reality which poetry and art can embellish. Our psalms and traditional prayers are more often than not wonderful poetry, but in reading them we must not imitate the actor. Reading prayers and reading poetry is never the same. The reader of poetry acts. This the worshipper must never do.

The reading of prayers, which brought the spoken word back to our worship, was a liturgical step which led beyond Hasidism and strengthened the prophetic Judaism of the modern synagogue. The prophet is a speaker. Who speaks, when the prophet speaks? God takes hold of the lips of a man, and while the man speaks his own word, it is the word of God. Endowed with the gift of speech, he has the possibility of praying. 'Blessed be God, who has not let my prayer and His love cease' (Ps. 66:20).

Psalm 66 makes it clear that man's prayer and the love of God are correlated. The Psalmist does not ask, 'Will my prayer be fulfilled?' He knows that prayer itself is fulfilment.

THE BOOK-READING WORSHIPPER

Christians have hymn books; Jews have their prayer book. Why do Jews not fold their hands when they pray? They cannot do so, because they are holding their prayer books. Nor do Jews kneel when praying, except during the Day of Atonement service. Of this fact the humanist will approve. His approval is appropriate. The Jew does not agree with the Christian view that the truest prayer is that arising out of human breakdown. Man can pray in happiness and in distress. The praying Jew stands upright before God; the Jew remains proud of his human status while praying. Jews prayed in concentration camps and at the stake of the Inquisition. But to establish Jewish divine service in the regulated form of the synagogue presupposes the possession of freedom. Slaves do pray – how profound are the Negro spirituals! But Jews pray as the slaves redeemed from Pharaonic bondage. A synagogue service has the atmosphere which prevails in the parliament of a free people. Only on the Day of Atonement, when the liturgy commemorates the one moment of the year in which the High Priest pronounced the ineffable name of God, the Jew does what he refused to do before the king of Persia and what no power on earth can compel him to do: he kneels.

The Jew, like the Christian and the Muslim, is an offspring of the monotheistic faith in which man expresses himself in prayer. The praying Jew is a 'book-reading worshipper'. Reading his prayers, the Jew is an intellectual man, but an intellectual man who prays. Both the Christian and the Christian humanist look upwards; they are uplifted, helped by art in the conversion of their human existence into a spiritual state. The Jew does not need this conversion. Praying, he looks forward to 'the world to come'. With his *kaddish* he praises the kingdom of God to come. This prayer brings the far-off day near to the Jew and makes it a reality which he praises in the sober attitude of a man reading about facts. The Jew at prayer looks forward. The distinction between 'this world' and 'the world to come' makes his prayer a Jewish prayer, whereas the Alexandrian distinction between the 'world below' and the 'world above' makes the Christian's prayer a Christian prayer.

Prayer is sacrifice offered as 'fruits of the lips' (Isa. 57:19). What does a man do in a house of worship? He does nothing. Doing is creating. While praying, man is not a creator, but a creature; he has brought the sacrifice to forgo his birthright of being what God is – a creator. God alone is Creator, but man, because he is created in the image of God, can be creative man. While praying, man has given up what he always enjoys doing; he is no longer creative man. He says: 'I know that I am dust and ashes' (Gen. 18:27), a creature of God. That is so with Jews, Christians and Muslims. But the Jew as a 'book-reading worshipper' is, while praying, still engaged in the most creative activity of man, which he shares with the humanist: he reads. A book, a work of creative man, binds man to his God and to his fellow-man. Jewish worship has its intellectual side. The Jewish House of Prayer is called *shool*, *schola*, place of study. The gentile's sacrifice is self-immolation. The sacrifice of the Jew, the book-reading worshipper, is brought by him as intellectual man. Reading his prayers which demand his intellectual attention, the praying Jew is both creator and creature.

Prayer is also the adoration of the miracle which surrounds man in the universe daily, 'every evening and morning', and also of that miracle which breaks into the history of man, as described in the biblical narrative about the rescue of Israel at the Red Sea. The precondition of any prayer is the belief in the possibility of miracles. The belief in miracles is implicit in belief in God. Belief in God comes first. We believe without 'a sign' from heaven (Isa. 7:11), without a proof of the truth of our belief. In the medieval hunt for 'holy relics', on the other hand, the relic had to be first; it caused belief in God. Belief was shaped by things touchable and visible, by events confirmed by eye-witnesses. This kind of belief is not belief, but superstition and ignorance, which give the medicine-man, the magician and the 'miracle rabbi' of decadent Hasidism their chance of profitable business, exploiting simple people. A miracle is one thing, a strange spectacle another – to refer to the medieval scholastics, who distinguished between *miraculum* and *spectaculum* (*theatron*, I Cor. 4:9). The rabbis of the Talmud restricted the prayers for 'the needs of the individual' (health, prosperity, forgiveness of sins) to the week-day service; in the sabbath benedictions the prayer book omits them. Furthermore, to the politician who became a zealot these rabbis of our classical, the Talmudical, age said: 'One does not rely on miracles.'

It is stupid to say that miracles never happen today. They only ever happen 'today' (or, we trust, in the future: we do not die into the grave, we die into the eternity of God). The miracles which have happened in the past are exposed to explanation, and an explained miracle is no longer a miracle; it has lost its immediacy, its verification in the existential experience of man saved by the miracle, blessed by the miracle. In a moment of joy the mother of a child who only yesterday was dangerously ill exclaims: 'A miracle has happened, the child will live and will be well again.' Afterwards, the miracle which made the mother a happy mother can be explained: the doctor's diagnosis was right, and he prescribed the right medicine.

The Jews, guided by their prayer book, praise the miracle at the Red Sea in their daily prayer. This miracle can be explained. 'The east wind probably swept bare the ford in the Red Sea hundreds of times and will do so again hundreds of times. But that it did this at a moment, when the people in their distress set foot in the sea – this is the miracle' (Rosenzweig, 1927, pp. 193–4). In the case of the miracle of the Battle of Britain an explanation is also at hand. It was all military logistics: Churchill, by giving orders to bomb Berlin, drew Hitler away from the airfields of the Battle of Britain fighters, the last few left. In 1940 civilization was saved by a miracle.

The miracle-stories circulating among the Hasidim kindled enthusiastic piety. Both the narrator and the listening circle create the atmosphere, in which the miracle reported in the story is apprehended as possible. The following example is typical of Hasidic life: A rabbi whose grandfather was a disciple of the Baal Shem, was asked to tell a story about him. He began:

> My grandfather was lame. Once, asked to tell something about the Baal Shem, he told the people that the Baal Shem, when praying, used to dance. While telling his story, my grandfather rose from his seat and his own story inspired him so much that he could not refrain from dancing himself to show how the master did it. From that moment he ceased to be lame.

No relics, nothing visible, no *theatron* created the Hasidic belief in miracles. It was created by words alone, by words spoken by Hasidim who told their stories and exchanged them with those of other Hasidic circles. 'Ye heard the voice of words, but ye saw no form; only a voice.' As long as this warning of Deuteronomy 4:12 was heeded by the Hasidim, their piety was Jewish piety.

Of course, Hasidism had its many miracle-stories, some edifying, some crude and repulsive. it is in each case a question of the literary success or failure of the narrator. Buber, himself a master of the craft of writing, collected what seemed to him valuable literature. Yet to take the miracle-stories of the Hasidim as literature and judge it as either good or bad literature is a wrong approach. It is Buber's approach. He edits that material which he considers worthy of being praised as a creation of Jewish culture. The real question is entirely different. Have the Hasidic miracle-stories the same directness as the miracle-stories of the Bible? There it is God who performs miracles. The man who attempts to do so or allows himself to be approached as capable of doing so, is a magician. The ignorant woman who brings her sick child to the rabbi-saint, to be healed by the touch of his hand or by a *quittel* (a ticket with a verse of the Bible written on it) is involved in the sin of magic of which the Hasidic rabbi is guilty. How often did such blasphemy occur in the Hasidic sector of Eastern European Jewry! Buber is silent, where the *Mithnaggdim* accuse a decadent Hasidism of a flourishing business, which exploited simple people in their belief in miracles.

Rabbi Immanuel Carlebach, a chaplain in the German army of occupation, describes the lavish wedding feast, which such a Hasidic rabbi arranged for a big crowd of guests in the starving Warsaw of 1917 (see Weltsch, 1961, vol. 6). Rabbi Carlebach did not realize that he was reporting a most despicable scene for posterity: the rich Hasidic rabbi, celebrating in front of hungry gentiles and bringing to his table his equally destitute followers. This scene is far removed from the Baal Shem, and the reader can only feel disgusted.

Hasidic rabbis were for a long time unable to find their way to the Talmud. It took two or even more generations before they sent their sons to the seats of Talmudic learning. In Hasidism the rabbinical office had become hereditary. For a hereditary office the credentials of learning are not required. The Baal Shem and the Hasidim of his time were not scholars.

Today the historical circumstances of Eastern European Jewry, which made Hasidism the first contribution of Ashkenazic Jewry to the revival of Judaism, are all past. In this outdated form Hasidism is still affirmed by the Jewish agnostic, for whom Tertullian's *credo, quia absurdum* (I believe, because it is paradox) provides the only door leading to Judaism. If one does not really pray to the God of Abraham, Isaac and Jacob, one can still sing Hasidic tunes and enjoy reading Buber's *Tales of the Hasidim*, and imagine that with that one is a Jew. Enthusiasts who recommend folk dances, such as the *Hora*, as Jewish culture also point to an outdated Hasidism, which made dancing the main constituent of ecstatic prayer. But the Hasidism which saw in prayer the centre of Jewish faith is never outdated.

Buber's writings about Hasidism refer to Hasidic doctrines. There are none. Buber's Hasidic doctrines are his own humanist doctrines, which he tries, usually unsuccessfully, to transform into classical Judaism, the Judaism of the prophets and rabbis. Early Hasidism was great in its practice, not in its doctrine. The efforts to formulate doctrines, so impressive in our Jewish scholastics, Saadia, Maimonides and Judah ha-Levi, to mention only the greatest, ceased with the end of the creative life of Sephardic Jewry. Doctrinal studies started again after a gap of

centuries in the movement which led German Jewry from Mendelssohn to Hermann Cohen, Leo Baeck and Franz Rosenzweig.
In this movement Martin Buber has a place. But as even Franz
Rosenzweig has in his doctrines to be critically reviewed as a
man before the holocaust of our time, so has Martin Buber to
be studied in a critical way.

FROM *DIN* TO RITUAL

The word *din* – to quote the *Shorter Encyclopaedia of Islam* (see
Gibb and Kramers, 1953, p. 77) – is 'an Arabic word meaning
"custom, usage"'. True, it is in Arabic an Aramaic-Hebrew
loan word; but the *Encyclopaedia* assures us that it is a 'genuine
Arabic word'. The Jew who asks 'What is the *din?*' has not yet
progressed from the Sephardic to the Ashkenazic chapter of
Jewish history. 'All aspects of public and private life should be
regulated by laws', says the Muslim (ibid., p. 102); orthodox
Jews would say 'by the *din*'. In this attitude they are still influenced
by Islamic civilization and its identification of law with religion.

The Jew guided in his performance of rituals by the codifiers
of the *din* responded with the obedience due to law. The word
Islam means unquestioning submission. The Muslim obeys laws.
This is his piety. Hasidism demanded a response with personal
approval, with 'inwardness'. Pietism and Hasidism reject the
medieval piety which makes praying and the performance of a
ritual an *opus operatum*, not less, but, alas, not more. This kind
of obedience becomes apparent in the formula: he is *yotse* (short
for *yotse hovato*), 'he has done his duty'. Everything is correct and
the absence of *kavanah*, of personal free motivation, does not
devalue the completed formality.

Moses Mendelssohn always made *havdalah*, performed the
ritual of ending the Sabbath and of welcoming the coming week.
In winter, the Sabbath ended early, when the guests, nobles
and intellectuals were in the *salon*, for tea and conversation. At
this moment Mendelssohn and his family withdrew for a few

minutes to a back room and there, where no guests disturbed their privacy, *havdalah* was made. Mendelssohn was not the man to hide his Jewish faith; his whole life is proof of this. But he is the medieval Jew who thought what was demanded of him was obedience to a law, and he strictly observed it. It did not occur to Mendelssohn that *havdalah* could be made not out of duty, but in enjoyment. Duty is duty, people say. Duty can be performed even without enjoyment. When performing a ritual – as when saying a prayer – we are involved in a way which is different from involvement in a duty. We should be able to perform a ritual not only like a prayer but also like a confession of faith, and a confession of faith is a public confession. Mendelssohn did not know what a ritual was, just as he did not know what gaslight or electricity was. From a religious point of view Mendelssohn still lived in the Middle Ages.

The German language forced a new word on Mendelssohn: *Zeremonialgesetz* (ceremonial law), a word which combines the two words ritual and law. He used it but was not aware that this very word, by distinguishing between ritual and law, could have shown the way out of the Middle Ages. On the contrary, he guarded himself against the implied meaning of this word. To him the *Zeremonialgesetz*, the law concerning a ritual, was revealed law, revealed on Mount Sinai. In this respect Mendelssohn is like a Muslim to whom the Koran is not a book, written by man, but a book from heaven, brought down by the archangel to Mohammed. Mendelssohn's 'revealed law' and the Muslim's 'revealed book' belong to the same category of medieval thinking. This complete absence of any critical attitude towards the facts of history startles us today, but this is the true Mendelssohn. He said: 'History bores me' (see Cassirer, 1929). Mendelssohn's 'revealed law' meant eternal law. He could regard laws, rituals, customs as revealed, i.e. eternal, because of his blindness towards history. The Muslim, while praying, turns to eternity. He craves for eternity, as the Christian craves for spirituality. The Muslim wants from history what history cannot give: eternity. Medieval man, above all the Muslim, speaks of eternal institutions, eternal laws, eternal customs. They are only holy to him when their unchangeability is established. But history is always change, is always an interim period. The prophets knew it. Modern Jewish Orthodoxy, upholding the unchangeability of all laws concerning Jewish rituals, forgets it.

Hasidism introduced only one new ritual: the Third Sabbath Meal. With the introduction of only one new ritual, all the old forms of piety, standardized by the *din*, begin to lose their super-human, inhuman, ikon-like grandeur, they lose their legal sanction and themselves become rituals. In medieval Jewry, influenced by Islamic civilization, reform, change, movement within the historic process, all progress in fact, found no sanction. The Islamic argument was that God is eternal, and everything in the history of man, if it is to be the way of Allah, must also have the seal of eternity; the holy law is eternal law, and any change would be an infringement of its holiness. The history of Western man is emancipation from the Middle Ages with their predominance of Islamic culture. The history of the West is a history of revolution, of reform, of change.

The situation in the Christian and Jewish world before the leavening influx of Pietism was ripe for the revolt against scholasticism and casuistry. Here is an example from the Christian camp. G. R. Cragg (1962, p. 100) writes:

> A seventeenth century sermon on Matthew 10, 30 ('But the very hairs of your head are all numbered') illustrates the arid formalism which did service for Christian truth. The divisions were as follows: (1) the origin, style, form and natural position of our hair; (2) the correct care of the hair; (3) reminiscences, reminders, warnings and comfort derived from the hair; (4) how to care for the hair in a good Christian fashion and to make use of it.

The lifeless pedantry of Lutheran orthodoxy has its parallel in the decadent rabbinic legalism, which characterizes for instance the responsa of Rabbi Meir of Lublin (died 1616). This head of a Talmudical High School (*Yeshivah*), known as the Maharam, published his learned papers about *halachot* of the Talmud from which the following sample is quoted: Is a woman guilty of adultery if the circumstances are such that the intercourse took place with the devil who appeared to the woman in the apparition of (a) her husband, (b) the Polish *Pan* (squire)? In very long and subtle discussions Maharam investigates whether this case should be dealt with according to the laws concerning adultery or concerning sodomy. In each case the consequences for the woman would be different. The result of the long, hair-splitting legal definitions has a happy ending; the woman is an adulteress only if adultery has been committed with a living person. The intercourse with a ghost who appears in human form cannot rob the husband of his honour, and the woman is, therefore, not an adulteress.

Aryeh Loeb, head of the Yeshivah of Minsk, and subsequently Rabbi in Metz in 1766, is also an example of the sad decline of rabbinical learning. He is known under the name 'Sha-agath Aryeh' (Roaring of the Lion), the title of his book in which he deals at length on how a left-handed man should put on his *tefillin*. His expositions of casuistry were learnt by heart by thirteen-year-old boys who recited them in their public oration (*derashah*) on the day of their *Bar Mitsvah*. In the name of religious instruction mental acrobatics were forced on these children, who had to find their way through a labyrinth of sentences in which the words 'left side', 'right hand', 'left hand', 'right side' were continuously interchanged. Rabbis of the type of Sha-agath Aryeh were numerous in Lithuania, that part of Eastern Europe into which Hasidism never penetrated owing to the zealous watch of the Gaon of Vilna.

It was out of the Jewish and Christian traditionalism of the seventeenth century that Pietism was born. Lutheran orthodoxy and the rabbinic pedantry of *pilpul* and *hilluk* (casuistry and sophistry) called for protest. The Hasidic protest rose against this lifeless and unbending orthodoxy. When we compare the Baal Shem with the Maharam and the Sha-agath Aryeh, we can say that the Baal Shem was human, and the two rabbis were not. Casuistry has been defended as a form of kindness; it tries to find a way out where there is none. But we must also heed the warning: 'Casuistry destroys, by distinctions and exceptions, all morality' (Bollingbroke). The Maharam and the Sha-agath Aryeh were rabbis of a decadent period. They uprooted laws from their historical basis so that what was once reasonable became nonsensical.

In the Middle Ages both Christianity and Islam aimed at a civilization unifying mankind. They aspired to the One World by working for the One Church or for the one world organization embracing all believers in Allah. Medieval political thinking conformed to Christianity and Islam by propagating the One *Reich*, the Holy Roman Empire. The codifiers of the *din* also lived in this religio-political atmosphere. They too wanted unity, that of the Jewish people. A Jewish ritual should be performed in the same way in North Africa and in Poland, Spain and Germany. Sephardic and Ashkenazic Jewry should be united by the *din*. The prophets looked towards a unity of mankind. They hoped for and insisted on a unity in which 'The wolf shall dwell with the lamb, and the leopard shall lie down with the kid; and the calf and the young lion and the fatling together; and a little child shall lead them' (Isa. 11:6). All the codifiers of the *din* could, as Jews, certainly fathom the profound hope of the prophets and they cherished it themselves. But in their work as codifiers they did not attempt to make it articulate.

How strongly the *din* directed medieval piety can be amplified by a humorous story. Rabbi Moses Isserles (1520–72), known as the Rema, codified all the *dinim* and added his amendments (*hagahot*) to the code of Joseph Caro, first published in 1564 in Venice. The authority of the Rema was high throughout Ashkenazic Jewry. Somewhere in a Polish city – so our story goes – people suffered from an exceptionally high number of pickpockets; the saying there was: 'It is a pity that the Rema did not make it a *din* not to steal.' Thus it was assumed that what a commandment of the decalogue could not achieve, the *din* could.

RITUALS AS GESTURES OF LOVE*

Hasidism had an important place in Judaism but must not become

* Hallo translates this phrase as 'the sign language of the love for God' (*Star*, p. 216).

identified with the whole of Judaism. Rituals have their place in Jewish life, but a ritualism, a religious life reduced to the performance of rituals, robs Judaism of its depth. The priest alone is not capable of guiding man. At the side of the priest must stand the prophet.

The prophet Amos is the most radical critic of a religious life corrupted by ritualism. 'I hate, I despise your feasts, and I will take no delight in your solemn assemblies' (Amos 5:21). Amos, like all other prophets before and after him, does not reject animal sacrifices. As a man of antiquity he approves of this way of worshipping God. With his stern words he rejects the piety of all ages, when it replaces morality, love and the care of one's neighbour. Pious men of all times are challenged by every biblical prophet. The numerous occasions when prayers are said and rituals are performed cannot be a substitute for what is really needed. 'Take thou away from Me the noise of thy songs; And let Me not hear the melody of thy psalteries. But let justice well up as waters, and righteousness as a mighty stream' (5:23, 24). These words should not be hurled against Hasidism. But anyone who prays, anyone who performs a religious ritual, must ask himself: do these words mean me?

Some kind of selection of the rituals that we inherited from the past became necessary. Because the rituals have to be performed with *kavanah*, with *hitlahavut*, they must be limited in number. Nor can rituals be made obligatory for post-medieval men. They cannot be dictated. They can be recommended. A modern code of rituals, a modern *shulchan aruch*, should be written – if it should be written at all – in the same way in which personal religious confessions are made. The writers should be like preachers. They would have to tell a generation biased against rituals how they have come to love rituals and how, through them, they are able to obey the commandment to love God. Rituals have to be explained as 'gestures of love'.

A Roman Catholic (see Guardini, 1922) says of the performance of a ritual that it is 'aimless, but significant'. This seems more a condemnation than a justification. J. Huizinga (1970) recognized at once that Guardini's 'aimless, but significant' is the very definition of – play. In the eyes of Plato, of any philosopher who replaces religion with an aesthetic approach, the comparison of the performance of a ritual with play is not blasphemous. Plato's 'All is play' can argue that in play there is something 'at play' which transcends the immediate need of life and imparts meaning to the action (Huizinga, pp. 1, 4, 19, 25). Plato's philosophy shows proximity to the prophetic faith, when he states that 'God alone is worthy of supreme seriousness' (*Laws* VIII, 3), but also reveals the unbridgeable gulf between his aesthetic religion and Judaism when he says in the same sentence: 'Man is God's plaything, and that is the noblest part of him. Therefore, every man and woman should live life accordingly and play the noblest games, and be of a different mind from what they are at present.'

A man performing a ritual transcends to a meaning beyond reality. So far we can agree with Plato. But shall we suggest that the Roman Catholic priest at his altar performing the rites of sacrifice according to prescribed rules is playing a game – a noble game, as Plato would call it. Guardini's definition of the ritual 'aimless, but significant' would be in line with this suggestion. Shall we suggest that the Jew lifting up the *kiddush* cup and breaking bread at his table, which is his altar, is playing a game? We shudder at such an explanation. But we must guard ourselves against allowing rituals to become mere play, just as we prevent our prayer from becoming a mere mumbling of words. Huizinga's indictment 'play' is a warning we should keep in our minds. He writes:

The spirit of the Middle Ages, still plastic and naive, longs to give concrete shape to every conception. Every thought seeks expression in an image, but in this image it solidifies and becomes rigid. By this tendency to embodiment in visible forms all holy concepts are constantly exposed to the danger of hardening into mere externalism.

Even in the case of a sublime mystic like Henry Suso the craving for hallowing every action of daily life verges in our eyes on the ridiculous. He is sublime when, following the usages of profane love, he celebrates New Year's Day and May Day by offering a wreath and a song to his betrothed, Eternal Wisdom, or when, out of reverence for the Holy Virgin, he renders homage to all woman-kind and walks in the mud to let a beggar woman pass. But what are we to think of what follows? At the table Suso eats three quarters of an apple in the name of the Trinity and the remaining quarter in commemoration of 'the love with which the heavenly Mother gave her tender child Jesus an apple to eat'; and for this reason he eats the last quarter with the paring, as little boys do not peel their apples. After Christmas he does not eat it, for then the infant Jesus was too young to eat apples. He drinks in five draughts because of the five wounds of the Lord, but as blood and water flowed from the side of Christ, he takes his last draught twice. This is, indeed pushing the sanctification of life (through rituals) to extremes (Huizinga, 1924, pp. 153–4).

After reading this passage a Jew might think of the New Year *kiddush* as we observe it in our homes. After *kiddush* and the blessing over the bread are said, a piece of apple is dipped into honey, and we say two benedictions: 'Blessed art Thou, O Lord, our God, King of the universe, who createst the fruit of the tree', and after having eaten the apple with the honey: 'May it be Thy will, O Lord, our God and God of our fathers, to renew unto us a happy and pleasant [literally 'sweet'] year.' After the various stages of this ceremony the festive meal begins.

What guarantee is there that this observance is far removed from what can be called play? There is no guarantee. With every ritual there is the risk that it can become an empty form, not only meaningless but also ridiculous. Only conscious and faithful devotion to the meaning of the ritual gives a human action the power to sanctify reality.

THEOLOGY VERSUS MYSTICISM

I mentioned earlier the significant fact that in the second edition of his *Die chassidischen Bücher* Buber crossed out the word 'ecstatic' where it was used as an attribute of Hasidism. This does not mean that Buber, having been a mystic, recanted and stopped being one. He himself never was a mystic; he was a connoisseur of mystical literature. In accordance with the literary atmosphere in which he sensed an unfavourable opinion of what he had called ecstatic religions, he no longer recommended Hasidism as a mystical movement to which the attribute 'ecstatic' could have applied. But the abandonment of the word 'ecstatic' was a gesture which was hardly noted by the generation which hailed Hasidism as a mystical movement. Understood in this way Hasidism can transform Jews, that is a community of individuals, into a collective group of the mass age. Should Jews be brought back into that cohesion of collective life from which the Emancipation had liberated them?

In wide circles of the Jewish generation after World War I Martin Buber and Gershom Scholem created a Jewish opinion which branded the anti-mysticism of the historian Heinrich Graetz as iconoclasm. Asked what 'mystical' means, a young Jew gave me the following answer: 'very religious'. With this reply the youngster shows himself to be the true representative of a generation brainwashed by Buber and Scholem. That Buber and Scholem themselves hold views on mysticism, which are often subtle and not at all primitive, is besides the point. The sad fact is that they are both responsible for the turn towards an irrationalism which hailed the mystic as an equal of the biblical prophet. The lights went out in the tents of Judah, too. Discursive thinking came to an end. The generation around Buber held the mystic in high esteem. Eventually the mystic became the guide for those who were ready to opt out from civilization.

In defence of Scholem it should be said that he is after all the historian of Jewish mysticism; his subject-matter happens to be mysticism. But a historian cannot avoid value-judgments. Scholem never utters any criticism of his mystics. Ortega y Gasset (1967, pp. 62-9) writes in his short but profound survey of Christian mysticism: 'The mystic is a madman.' Scholem never warns against mysticism. His objectivity as a scholar has created a great public which, through him, believes in mysticism. Scholem's learned catalogue of mystical manuscripts and mystical terminology ('sparks', *tzimtzum*, that is the withdrawal of God into himself, *sefirot*, Kabbala, Zohar) could often be truly characterized by the word 'rubbish'. This word, redeeming as it would be, like Ortega y Gasset's 'madman', is not spoken by Scholem.

That Plotinus and Meister Eckhart were great thinkers does not invalidate the judgment that calls the mystic a madman. These two great men were thinkers besides their being mystics. As mystics they are not different from other vulgar ecstatics.

The aim and the technique of the mystics is always the same, whether we consider Alexandrian or Arabic mystical books, which influenced Jewish mystics, or whether we turn to Indian or Chinese, Teutonic or Spanish ones. There is no difference in the essential points, the experts assure us. The aim is to empty one's consciousness of any content; the way to achieve this is to gaze at one fixed point.

There is never a mystical trance without a mental vacuum. 'That is', says St John of the Cross, 'why God commanded the altar where sacrifices were to be made to be empty inside . . . so that the soul will realise how empty God wishes it to be of all other things.' The Indian mystic lights a fire, places a screen before it in which he makes a hole, and looks at the light coming through.

The amazing thing is, that once the mind is cleared, so the mystic assures us, he has God before him; God consists of precisely that vacuum. Eckhart speaks of 'the silent desert of God', St John of the Cross of 'the dark night of the soul'. He also describes this complete vacuum as 'sonorous solitude'. God filters into the soul and merges with it or, we are told, the soul dilutes into God and no longer feels that He is a different being from itself. The *unio mystica* has happened. What in fact did happen? Man has ceased to be a person, he has become a 'sponge of divinity'. 'Sponge of divinity', 'automaton of God', mechanical 'puppet' which God controls, these are the words which occur time and time again in the language of the mystics. The distinction between the human person and God ends, the human person and God 'flow' into each other. This is the end of European personalism: it means a Europe swallowed up by Asia.

Let us turn away from the temptation of the mystics! They advise us to opt out from European civilization and to find salvation in Asia's religious nihilism. Let us be faithful to Europe and let us hope! The enrichment of our ideas about divine matters will not emerge from the mystics' subterranean paths. It will rise from the luminous path of discursive thought. Let us turn to theology, let us reject ecstasy!

CHAPTER II

Franz Rosenzweig – Today's Guide for the Perplexed

THE ISLAMIC GOWN OF JEWISH ORTHODOXY

The German Islamic scholar Karl Becker states that 'the gown which Christianity wore in the Middle Ages was woven in the orient'. The supremacy of Islamic culture over Christian culture in the Middle Ages is an established fact. Viewed from the high civilization of the Muslim cities of North Africa and Spain, Europe could be called – a Balkan country. But this cultural Islamic frame of both medieval Christianity and medieval Jewry must not allow us to forget that Christianity, Islam and Judaism are different. In a moving letter which he wrote in his old age to his Muslim pupil, the great Jewish Islamic scholar Ignaz Goldziher writes: 'We are brothers. We have the same God.' This is true. But as theologians we must be clear about the differences which a Jewish-Christian-Islamic trialogue must articulate for the benefit of the three monotheistic religions.

Hasidism shows the impact of Christian culture on Judaism. Hasidism is part of European Christian Pietism. Before the Hasidic chapter of Jewish history, in the geonic period and in the period of the codifying rabbis, Islamic cultural influence prevails. In fact during the whole of the Middle Ages there was no difference between Jews and Muslims in Christian eyes.

A historian who is an expert in these matters, says: 'had there been no great outburst of anti-Muslemism there would have been little if any antisemitism in the High Middle Ages' (Cutler, 1968, p. 472). Christianity has right from the beginning refused to acknowledge Islam as a monotheistic religion in its own right. For the Christian, Islam is a Christian heresy. This hostility between Christian and Muslim is significant for the Middle Ages; it is out of date in our post-medieval age. This does not mean that we should regard the difference between love and law, between book religion and prophetic religion lightly. It is a difference which makes Christian and Muslim the twins coming from Rebecca's womb, brothers, but brothers in doctrinal disagreement. The parable referring to the Jewish mother, to the womb of Rebecca, containing the still united brothers, who are not to be united in life, is significant. It is even more satisfactory than Judah Ha-Levi's parable of the seed bringing forth the tree with two branches, Christianity and Islam. Doctrinal differences between Christian and Muslim will remain unresolved on the dogmatic level. Yet what Christianity and Islam as organizations, as denominations, cannot unite can be united in the human existence of the Jew.

The controversy between progressive and orthodox Jews remains unresolved so long as it is not seen that Jewish Orthodoxy defends a position which is Islamic and not Jewish. The orthodox rabbis in Israel and in other parts of our diaspora are *ulema*, Islamic divines, rather than rabbis. Both in the Rabbinic Assemblies of 1844–8 and in the dialogue between Rosenzweig and Buber of 1923 the case of Progressive Judaism would have been much stronger had it been understood that Jewish Orthodoxy was still influenced by Islamic thinking. In the Rabbinical Assemblies of 1844–8 Rabbi Zacharias Frankel opposed the progressive Rabbi Abraham Geiger (1910, p. 300) with the statement: 'What is accepted by the community as custom, no authority can abrogate.' The statement of this rabbi is the exact formulation of what the Muslim calls *idjma*. Orthodox Judaism is defended with the help of an Islamic tenet. This is also the case in many other instances, as will be seen, when we turn to

Franz Rosenzweig's dialogue with Buber, as recorded in his pamphlet *The Builders* (1924), and to his other references to the controversy between the orthodox and progressive inter-pretation of Judaism.

Franz Rosenzweig writes about 'the law which cannot be abrogated by a revolution; one can run away from it but one cannot change it' (*Star*, p. 304). It is surprising that Rosenzweig describes Jewish law in these words. What he says here and – as we shall see – what he soon retracts, is the very description of the law as the Muslim understands it. The Muslim is convinced that he is in possession of a historic written law which is a 'revealed law'. *Sharia*, which includes the Koran, is indeed, in the opinion of the Muslim, 'the law from which one is able to run away, but which no man can change'. In the clashes with rulers and intellectuals the *ulema* could always point to the holy law which they had no power to change. Chief Rabbi Dr Jakobovits says to this day in London what the *ulema* said. The tradition, the *ulema* say, is established, innovation is neither desirable nor possible. Every traditionalist, be he Jew or Christian, will argue in the way of the Muslim who turns to the *hadith*, the pious search into transmitted traditions. He is persuaded that only there will he find the truth for which he searches. With its faithfulness to the existing tradition Islam could mix with various cultures, could soon absorb them and yet remain un-changed Islam.

It has been said: 'Pauline Christianity can become "faith in faith".' A faith in faith can cease to be faith in God. In adjust-ment to the new era created by Paul, the word Torah was translated for Greek-speaking man by the word *nomos*, which means law. But the protest against Paul's faith on a world his-toric scale did not come from the Jews. It came from Islam. The Torah is both law and doctrine; it has both its nomistic and anti-nomistic features. While the Christian tries to unfold again and again the content of faith as doctrine, it is the Muslim, not the Jew, who has rejected this spiritual enterprise. Let God be God. Not doctrinal search but obedience is due to Him. Here, where he should totally agree with the Muslim, Rosenzweig joins the

Christian and says that the formula 'God is God' (*alla il alla*) is a tautology. Christian theologians have said this throughout the centuries since the rise of Islam. Rosenzweig should have acknowledged the very nearness of this statement to, if not its identity with, our 'The Lord is One'. This is not an arithmetical statement. It tells all mankind in solemn triumph that no doctrinal subtlety and no prophetic metaphor can express what God is. 'Who is God?' a child asks when he hears of Him for the first time in a story narrated in the Bible or the Koran. The teacher, as a resolute pedagogue, answers: 'Don't be silly: God is God.' As adults we have become like silly children by not stopping to enquire, where we think enquiry is out of place. We too must be satisfied with the answer 'God is God'. Rosenzweig, one could argue, is guilty of the same 'tautology' of which he accuses the Muslim. He writes: 'The content of revelation is revelation.' Very well. But is this not also a 'tautology'? Muslim law and Christian revelation are as concepts both understood by the Jew, but are never wholly transferable to the situation of the Jew. The Christian knows the time and place of the one Revelation; the Jew, upholding prophetic Judaism, can only speak of revelations, in the plural. Every Jew must 'stand at Sinai' in his own lifetime. There is no biblical Hebrew word for revelation. The Hellenistic Jew who translated the Hebrew Bible into Aramaic found 'He came down' too anthropomorphic and translated 'He revealed himself', creating a new word, revelation, for the vocabulary of mankind.

The holy law of the Muslim and the faith of the Pauline pattern, faith in the one revelation, became the two irreconcilable forms of monotheism. Judaism recognizes the two opposing partners, Islam and Christianity, as blood from its own blood, and flesh from its own flesh. But Judaism remains different from either of them. To understand Judaism as 'religion of law' is to misunderstand it. It is to identify Judaism with Islam. This has been done by Christian theologians in the past and is still done today.

Rosenzweig acknowledges only Judaism and Christianity as monotheistic religions. He does not acknowledge Islam as monotheism. This is a mistake, but when a man of the stature of Rosenzweig makes a mistake, there is still a lot left to learn from him. Rosenzweig sees Islam as 'Religion of Reason and Duty' and with this mistaken premise he is successful in grasping the true essence of the humanism of his time. This humanism was indeed a 'religion' of reason and moral duty. Protestant ethics and German philosophical idealism made this humanism a force of German bourgeois civilization. It cared for the welfare of man and believed in the regulative idea of a united mankind. It was belief in man. It was not belief in God. It was not monotheism. Islam, as a religion of reason and moral duty, stemming from a belief in God, *is* monotheism.

The dispute between Jewish Orthodoxy and Progressive Judaism has so far – to say the least – always led to a stalemate. Christian or Islamic doctrines are used in the controversy. But those who argue with the help of these doctrines are unaware that they defend not Judaism, but Christian or Islamic thoughts and behaviour which have penetrated Jewish life. Emancipation from the Middle Ages means emancipation from medieval Christian and Islamic culture. Reform Judaism is today the refusal to go on wearing 'the gown woven in the orient'. In rejecting the rabbi who teaches what the *ulema* teach, the Jew is not merely a Western Jew, but a Jew emancipated from a past which has become meaningless. But we cannot turn to a kind of Jewish doctrine and with it oppose Islamic law and Christian doctrine. Such a Jewish doctrine, which pronounces *ex cathedra* the Jewish point of view against Christianity and Islam, does not exist. Instead we must put forward our Jewish approval or disapproval step by step. Above all we must always see ourselves involved as Jews when Christianity and Islam are under critical investigation. Judaism must regard the two other monotheistic religions as its descendants and as fellow-fighters. All the three monotheistic religions must unite to combat the dark age which threatens our civilization.

In Islam the formula 'as it is written' has a sacrosanct character. Here Rosenzweig's hostility to Islam makes him see its difference from a Judaism in which the prophetic elements are alive. A

47

prophetic understanding of Judaism prevents it from becoming a book-religion. Our faithful, unending study of the Holy Scriptures to be pursued by young and old, does not let us lapse into book-idolatry. Rosenzweig writes: 'Should God residing in His high heaven have to give man – a book?' (*Star*, p. 166).

The Muslim, not the Jew, has a 'holy book'. The *Tenach* (the Hebrew Bible) is not *biblos* (the Greek word for book). Not 'holy book' but 'holy books' is the term in Jewish tradition. The Sadducees upheld the Torah as a closed book and guarded it against any contamination from additional interpretation. But our Judaism is Pharisaic Judaism. The Pharisaic doctrine of the 'oral tradition' is a mere fiction but it became a blessing: it opened the door through which new ideas, new interpretations, new customs and new laws could enter and become – Torah. The Pharisees succeeded in preventing the Torah from shrinking into mere books. The Torah is not a book in the sense of the Koran. Nor must revelation be understood by Jews in the Christian sense as an event which took place at one time (in the year one) and at one place (in Palestine). 'God came down', as recorded in Exodus 19:20, is the content of revelation; the words which follow, 'upon Mount Sinai' and 'The Lord said to Moses', are already *midrash*, pious narrative, interpretation of the revelation, not the revelation itself. 'God came down': man does not need more than these three words. In these three words he has – revelation.

The tradition recorded in the Talmud must not be identified with *sunna* (the unchangeable path to be trodden by the Muslim). The Talmud can be called a 'Hansard': free men discuss their problems, and the Talmudic Hansard reports them from the second century to the sixth. In the Talmud we still breathe the air of the polis, of the city with its free citizens. The Muslim never experienced freedom. He knew the difference between master and slave. But the fight for freedom, in which the Popes rose against the emperors, has no equivalent in the history of Islam. In Western civilization's passionate concern for freedom Islam does not participate. In this, Islam is the pattern for all forms of totalitarianism. Whether happy and content in the benevolent tribal democracy, or suffering under the cruel authoritarianism of sultans and feudal lords, the Muslim must do without freedom. In their submission to God Muslims do not see themselves as 'children of God' but as slaves of God. Where Jewish Orthodoxy succeeds in establishing community life, the members of the flock are denied freedom of thought, and the authority of the rabbi has to be acknowledged like that of the *ulema*.

The sermon plays a great role in synagogue, church and mosque. The sermon interprets texts and doctrines, demands commitments of various forms and presents moral admonition. But where laws are proclaimed as holy laws, the man who speaks to a congregation becomes a legal scholar rather than a preacher. Nevertheless, the mosque had its pulpit, and sermons were preached there. This was most of all the case with the *Sufis*, the Islamic sect which was more under Christian influence than Islam as a whole. It was in the Jewish communities of Eastern Europe, in the time between the expulsion from Spain and the rise of Hasidism, that the sermon was neglected and that the rabbis became similar to the *ulema*. When progressive Jews in Berlin introduced the sermon into their divine services, orthodox rabbis complained to the government about Jewish heresy. Their point was that the sermon is right for the church, but not for the synagogue. At that time the elders of the Berlin Jewish Community commissioned Leo Zunz (1794–1886) to write a learned essay about the sermon. He proved that the sermon had always flourished in the classical periods of Jewish history. It was a sign of decadence that the Eastern European rabbi refused to preach, regarded it beyond his dignity as a legal scholar to do so, and left the preaching to the *maggid*, who was popular but seen as possessing a lower status than the rabbi.

Leo Zunz was for the Rosenzweig family a kind of family saint. But Rosenzweig did not agree with Zunz when he wrote: 'As long as the Talmud is not dethroned, nothing can be done.' This was the view of the Jewish Enlightenment movement. Rosenzweig already lived in the light which the great historians of the nineteenth century bestowed on a new generation. Guided by these historians they moved away from the Middle Ages. The *Wissenschaft des Judentums*, that vigorous and creative offspring of German historiography, dissolved the Talmudic block into its many parts. The historic, linguistic, doctrinal and legal parts became separated from each other and modern Talmudic study lost the dreariness and abstruseness which had made Zunz, taught in his youth by the old unpedagogic method of his masters, despair. Today the Talmud is a valuable source-book. It has been demythologized by the historian. The progressive Jew, who has shed the medieval gown woven in the orient, sees the Talmud without any numinous quality. It could never claim such quality. In the past we had the Babylonian Talmud and the Palestinian Talmud. Today we have our European Talmud, to be found in the many books written in German, English and modern Hebrew. The progressive rabbis have emancipated us from the Islamic concept of the 'holy book'.

Montgomery Watt, an authority on Islam, points to the danger of the 'fixational' attitude of Islam. 'The conservative attitude loses its justification and becomes fixational, if it goes so far that an adjustment to changed circumstances becomes too difficult. Most religions were in some periods of their history too conservative.' The post-Talmudic literature becomes a literature of 'commentaries on commentaries'. A lack of creative new formulation becomes characteristic of Islam after the canonization of the Koran. The Jewish literature of the geonic period and of the period of the codifying rabbis is also devoid of any creative element. Tradition becomes fixation to the past, making any adaptation to a new situation impossible. A fixational attitude leads to the fundamentalism from which the Jewish people, deprived since the holocaust of numerous scholars, suffers today. The civilized Orthodoxy of what was once German Jewry has become primitive, narrow-minded fundamentalism. Rosenzweig's pamphlet *The Builders*, written ten years before the outbreak of the catastrophe of 1933, gives for the last time an intelligent exposition of the controversy between Orthodoxy and Progressive Judaism. But we have to enquire whether the dialogue between Buber and Rosenzweig, in which German Jewry participated, has still some meaning for us.

Rosenzweig, at the time of writing the *Star*, is a convert. He turns away from German philosophical idealism and becomes – a Jew. Entering his newly-acquired commitment to the world of Judaism, he is prepared to accept everything; he is unwilling to be critical about the difference between medieval and post-medieval Judaism. The difference is ignored. He encounters the term Jewish Law and is prepared to accept it. But even in the youthful fervour of his new discovery, in which he writes the *Star*, he distinguishes between commandment (*mitsvah*) and law (*Torah*). The *mitsvah* is action, performing a ritual. It is significant that the terminology is 'one performs a *mitsvah*', not 'one obeys a *mitsvah*'. The Jew who performs a *mitsvah* obeys a commandment which in some instances is of minor importance or of no importance at all and which is never legally binding. Rosenzweig criticizes not the Jewish Law, but the law of the Muslim, and the reader who studies the *Star* has to find out for himself, where Rosenzweig speaks of Jewish and where of Muslim law. It must be pointed out that a distinction between commandment (*mitsvah*) and law is not applicable to Islam. In Islam everything is law, the highest ethical commandment as well as some minor religious practice. On the other hand, Rosenzweig understands rituals as gestures of love. This concept contradicts the Christian theologian who – identifying Judaism with Islam – calls Judaism a religion of law, Christianity a religion of love. Unfortunately, Rosenzweig gave his pamphlet *The Builders* the subtitle 'About the Law'. The beautiful description of rituals as gestures of love is not considered. Rosenzweig suggested that Buber should enter the world of Jewish rituals. Buber – rightly – refused to accept rituals which were described to him as laws.

In the third part of his *Star* Rosenzweig deals with the calendar of the Jew. He describes life in the synagogue and in the family. It seems that Rosenzweig deals with the same material as the Shulchan Aruch, the code which is still regarded as authoritative for the orthodox Jew. Yet there is a decisive difference. Rosenzweig writes what has become his personal conviction. He demands nothing. He describes a way of life. He writes his confessions, the confessions of a modern Jew who has discovered Judaism of old. The Shulchan Aruch, on the other hand, is a book of law, just like any other law-code, which the Jew, like a Muslim, has to obey without asking questions. He has to obey not as autonomous man; he obeys by way of heteronomous allegiance. It is *the* Law, the Law of God.

Rosenzweig deals with questions like these. No doubt his view is his personal opinion, but it has a quality which no dry jurists can achieve. Those who accept Rosenzweig's description of Jewish life are invited to do so voluntarily and not with the unquestioning obedience of the orthodox Jew, who does, in the field of rituals, what the *din*, what the *halachah*, stipulates. Rosenzweig does not say in any one case 'You have to do it.' He only says 'You are able to do it.' He appeals to the autonomous man in the Jew. *Din* and *halachah* turn to the man of the Middle Ages who has not achieved the emancipation which could have made him an autonomous man. In our post-medieval age *din* and *halachah* foster Islamic rather than Jewish piety. *Halachah* has become identical with the Muslim's *sunna*, the way everybody is supposed to walk. An individual selection of rituals and thereby their reduction to a smaller number are out of the question with such an Islamic interpretation of *din* and *halachah*. Orthodox Judaism, influenced by Islam, accepts the dogma of the *ulema*: the doors of *ijtihad* (prophetic interpretation of tradition) are closed. For Rosenzweig they were not closed. Nor are they closed for any Jew of the progressive sector who has thrown away 'the gown woven by Islam'.

Two years after finishing the *Star* Rosenzweig emancipated himself from the Islamic interpretation of Jewish law. No longer did he see the Jewish Law as 'the Law which no revolution can change and from which one can run away, but which one cannot change'. Post-medieval Jewry had not run away from the laws and rituals which under the conditions of the Middle Ages had united the Jewish people, dispersed among many nations, into one closely knit community. Most of these laws and rituals had fallen away from the Western Jews like leaves falling from the trees in autumn. Rosenzweig acknowledged the new situation. He no longer spoke of Jewish Law without qualification, he spoke of the 'law of western Orthodoxy of the nineteenth century'.

Eventually Rosenzweig formulates: 'Judaism is *not* [his italics] law, Judaism creates law. But Judaism *is not* identical with law. Judaism "is" to be a Jew.' This is Rosenzweig's Copernican turn from medieval metaphysics concerning the Jewish Law to the Jew himself. The Jew as a 'peculiar' type of man is in the centre; 'Mount Sinai' and 'the *Torah* [Law] *from Heaven*' are de-mythologized. The two-thousand-year-old covenant with God depends on the fragile, embattled, persecuted, earthly figure of the Jew. No longer is the Torah understood as eternal Law, the guarantee. The Jew is the guarantor of the eternal Torah. The modern, post-medieval understanding of Jewish existence is already formulated in Isaiah's ' "My witnesses", says the Lord, "are you" ' (43:10).

The new situation is clearly apparent in our use of the word 'ritual'. Pre-modern man did not speak of rituals. A medieval Christian would have regarded it as blasphemous to call the performances of a Roman Catholic priest at the altar 'rituals'. To the Muslim, too, the minutiae of his pious behaviour – from his movements while praying to the rules for his pilgrimage to Mecca – were more than mere rituals. The pre-modern Jew performing the rituals demanded from him by the Shulchan Aruch, thought himself obedient to a law; he did not use nor did he even know the semantic formula of the word 'ritual'.

Rosenzweig describes the time in which we live today when he writes: 'The Jewish Law distinguishes today more between Jew and Jew than between Jew and gentile.' In this situation modern Jews ponder which rituals, how many or how few of them, they are obliged to perform. Rosenzweig's advice is: 'Try them out, do what you are able to do, but what you are able to do, do!' He also says that our inability to accept the obligation to perform some of the rituals, may be a true and genuine contribution to pious Jewish behaviour. Modern Jewry, however, began to reduce the number of rituals and to select from them those which were able to bring holiness into their lives.

Rosenzweig did not succeed in weaning Buber from a Judaism reduced to Jewish nationalism. Buber was acquainted with the piety of Poland, his birthplace, where Jewish rituals were alive as ethnic forms and as popular religion without individual reflection. Buber also rejected 'the law of western orthodoxy of the nineteenth century'. It was, he argued, not a national expression of the Jewish people; it represented only a congregation, the small band of men and women who followed Rabbi S. R. Hirsch as their pastor. Rosenzweig, on the other hand, was attracted by the pietistic warmth of the German orthodox Jewish communities. He criticized, though, the primitive theology of S. R. Hirsch. When Rosenzweig was acclaimed by orthodox speakers as a conservative or even as an orthodox theologian, he protested and said: 'I am a liberal Jew.' He was. He subscribed to the method of biblical criticism.

Like Rosenzweig in his youth, Hermann Cohen turned away in his old age from philosophical humanism and became a Jew in the true sense. He revealed to an orthodox rabbi his feelings about the few rituals which he performed. 'When I make *kiddush*, when I say *motsi*, when I say grace, I am so moved that tears come into my eyes.' The orthodox rabbi commented to me about Cohen's confession with the words: 'Why is he moved? When I make *kiddush* or say *motsi* or say grace, I do it to be *yotse*' (to fulfil my duty). Man shaped by autonomy and man of the heteronomic pattern are absolutely different, even when they seem to do the same thing. Heteronomic man still stands in the Middle Ages, autonomous man has left them. At the start of his theological pilgrimage Rosenzweig thought he could embrace the whole of Judaism by ignoring the difference between medieval and post-medieval Judaism and the difference between law and ritual. He therefore spoke of the Law which no revolution can abrogate and from which one can run away but which one cannot change. He later realized that with these words he had defined Islamic, not Jewish, law, not the Torah. Yet he soon found the one, unalterable, eternal Judaism, not to be changed in its essence in the course of history. He therefore spoke of an unalterable law, but in the end attached to it a different meaning. He saw Jewish existence as eternal existence, and the law constituting this existence as eternal and holy law.

In conclusion we may well ask: what is the *halachah*? The answer is simple: it is the path on which man walks (*halach*), heeding Micah 6:8: 'It hath been told thee, O man, what is good; and what the Lord requireth of thee: only to do justly, and to love mercy, and to walk humbly with thy God.' In his obedience to God the Jew is different from Christian and Muslim. Neither the faith in which Paul turned to God nor the Muslim's submission to the will of God is a prophetic attitude. But a prophetic attitude is needed. It is there in the Jewish people. A Jew hears the call which bids him to worship God and to obey Him. The Law of God is a call which demands that we be men walking with God.

IGNORANT ARMIES CLASHING BY NIGHT

The use of the attributes 'Orthodox', 'Liberal', 'Reform', 'Conservative', applied to the various sections of post-medieval Jewry, can often be discarded as unhelpful and even as misleading. In many cases this internal Jewish controversy is better understood when it is realized that Christian and Islamic thinking have penetrated Jewish life. The arguments of the warring sections of modern Jewry are supposed to come from the armoury of true, unadulterated Jewish tradition. But this is all too often not the case. An analysis according to the method of the history of ideas proves that the arguments with their labels, Orthodox, Liberal, Reform, Conservative, are feeble ideologies, which are no longer – if they ever were – convincing. Under the surface of these ideologies are the strong forces of Jewish, Christian and Islamic convictions. The modern Jewish factions are like 'ignorant armies (who) clash by night' (Matthew Arnold, 'Dover Beach'), since they do not know when an argument in their controversy is truly Jewish and when it is a Christian or an Islamic one deemed to be Jewish.

'Some people think our generation has to face a stormy day', wrote Teilhard de Chardin. 'They do not realise', he continued, 'that the climate of the world has changed.' Of this change Leo Baeck made his students aware, when, facing them at the beginning of their first term at the Hochschule, he told them that the Torah had been written like the works of Goethe or Shakespeare. In this dramatic way he expressed what the era of historical criticism means to the post-medieval generation. The Torah which the rabbis had seen as a pre-creation being, the Torah apprehended as Logos, as Son of God, the Torah, revered by Mohammed as 'book from heaven', as the Koran – all three, Torah, Christ, Koran, were reduced to relics by the scientfic criticism of the historian. Medieval man needed relics which could kindle his faith in God. The Middle Ages have gone. The climate of the world has changed. Searching for God, walking with God, we have no use for, and no need of, relics. History can provide only relics. It cannot provide the truth for which those who worship God crave, and which they themselves experience. A Copernican reorientation from history to man himself constitutes the post-medieval age. The Copernican reorientation moves from the Torah towards the Jew, who, shaped by prophetic Judaism, makes his decision here and now. The Copernican reorientation moves from Christ to the Christian, from the word written in the 'book from heaven', the Koran, to man acknowledging his obligation to do what is unalterably and eternally right. From Judaism, Christianity, Islam the Copernican reorientation moves towards the Jew, the Christian, the Muslim.

PAUL AND MOHAMMED

The rehabilitation of the Pharisees through Abraham Geiger, G. F. Moore, Travers Herford and Claude Montefiore shows Jewish law as being in harmony with prophetic Judaism. This rehabilitation does not include Islamic law, which is, as unalterable written law, devoid of the prophetic capacity of achieving innovation. The Pharisaic rabbis said: 'The oral law is older and holier than the written law.' The 'oral' law in this context is a legal fiction, but a most creative fiction. It preserved prophetic Judaism in rabbinic law. When the *ulema*, the Muslim divines, were approached by rulers or intellectuals to introduce an innovation, their standard answer was: 'I have no authority to change anything' or 'When you take out one small piece from the edifice of holy law, the whole system of law collapses'. W. Montgomery Watt who records this standard answer of the *ulema* in his book *What is Islam?* has hardly any idea that this is exactly what orthodox rabbis say today, not knowing that they are under the influence of Islam. Except within certain limits set by precedent, the *ulema* refuse to vary any application of the law. From the geonic period onwards rabbis had in assimilation to Islamic culture become *ulema*-rabbis.* When orthodox rabbis in Israel call a reform rabbi pastor or parson, the obvious reaction for the reform rabbi is to call the orthodox rabbi *ulema*-rabbi. The *ulema*-rabbi acts according to the Islamic doctrine, 'The gates of *ijtihad* are closed.' (After Mohammed, prophetic interpretation of tradition is no longer possible.) The rehabilitation of Pharisaic rabbinical Judaism as prophetic Judaism does therefore not refer to the concept of law accepted by the *ulema* or the *ulema*-rabbi. The great scholars who defended the Pharisees against the slur of the New Testament and showed them to be the equals of the prophets had no quarrel with Paul, in so far as he pleaded for the spirit of the law against the letter of the law. Paul's criticism of legalism is justified in regard to Islam and in regard to a Judaism assimilated to Islam. Modern Jews watching Galsworthy's play *Justice*, and seeing how in this play justice

* The formula '*ulema*-rabbi' has penetrated the Jewish controversy between Orthodox and Progressive rabbis. To an Islamic scholar the term '*ulema*-rabbi' is a grammatical monstrosity as *ulema* is a plural form and cannot be connected with a word in the singular. Even more decisive is the fact that in the last decades many *ulema* have demanded a 're-opening of the gates of *ijtiha* (an interpretation allowing an innovation of the law)' and are therefore Reform-*ulema*. The '*ulema*-rabbi' of the Jewish controversy refers to the medieval *ulema*. This footnote is meant as an apology for using the term '*ulema*-rabbi', which is accepted in Jewish circles.

becomes injustice in the name of the law, will agree with the author and therefore also follow Paul. What separates Jews from Paul is his conviction that the antithesis, spirit versus the written law, is irreconcilable; to a Jew shaped by prophetic Judaism it is reconcilable.

WITHOUT 'THE LEAP INTO FAITH'

As Western Jews we continually meet Paul. Since the time of Moses Mendelssohn we are Western Jews. In these one hundred and fifty years we have laboured to make Judaism theoretically articulate. We spoke of Jewish 'faith'. But faith is the cornerstone of Paul's theology. In the East, in the world of Islamic culture, law was the medium to express Judaism. In the West, when Jews approached the orbit of Christian civilization, doctrine became the medium to make Judaism articulate. The rabbis demonstrated their leadership by spreading a knowledge of the theoretical, historical, linguistic exposition of Judaism. Doctrine as knowledge turns to the intellect, creed does not. Doctrine is not creed. A creed has to be believed and belief, Paul's belief, is not to be expected from the Jew. Belief, Paul's belief, changes man. Believing, man becomes another man, a second Adam, a man changed from human to spiritual status. Faith lifts man into the spiritual sphere. The Tenach does not record in any place what Paul calls 'belief' or what he calls 'spirit' (*pneuma*).

Baeck's *Wesen des Judentums* (*The Essence of Judaism*, 1948), Franz Rosenzweig's *The Star of Redemption*, and the many treatises of previous German scholars, set out to give an exposition of Jewish doctrine drawn from the sources which modern Jewish history had made available. None of these scholars, whom the very fact of a Christian environment forced to formulate Jewish doctrine and to become theologians, intended to offer a Jewish creed as an answer to the Christian creed.

Emunah does not mean belief, it means firmness. *Bitachon* means trust. For Paul's *pistis*, belief, no equivalent Hebrew word exists. Rosenzweig could therefore write: 'The Jew does not believe in something, he is himself the belief' (*Star*, p. 342). Rosenzweig rejects Kierkegaard, this great Christian of the Pauline pattern. Kierkegaard observes the patriarchs and calls their way of life bourgeois. How is it that these people with good appetites and with their feet on the ground know of God, speak of God and walk with God? asks Kierkegaard. His answer points to what he calls 'the leap into faith'. The leap into faith is a leap into spiritual height. Faith and love, say all the Paulines, lift man into the realm of the spirit. Kierkegaard loves Regina, his fiancée, but he would not marry her. He wishes to remain in the realm of the spiritual with his love. He does not intend to consummate his love in marriage. He would not have been able to understand, and if he had understood them he would have rejected, Franz Rosenzweig and Gustav Landauer, who both, independently of each other, wrote the following sentence shining brightly like a heavenly star in their massive works of theological and political views: 'Marriage is more than love.'

Ortega y Gasset was, like Rosenzweig and Landauer, under the philosophical influence of the 'Marburg School' in which Hermann Cohen lectured. Ortega y Gasset wrote a profound book entitled *On Love*. Like Rosenzweig and Landauer, he wrote about the marital love which Kierkegaard rejected for himself and Regina: 'Love in which a human remains attached once and for all to another human being is a sort of metaphysical grafting.'

Professor Fackenheim uses the phrase 'leap into faith' in nearly every one of his theological essays. Professor Bergmann (Jerusalem) reprimanded me in a letter for not agreeing that there is a need to leap into faith. Rabbi Louis Jacobs calls the title of a learned book *We have Reason to Believe*. No: we have no reason to believe. We do not go the way of Paul, just as we do not go the way of Mohammed. We Jews are willing to accept that Christians, in the tension between faith and doubt, can be successful in their 'leap into faith'. But we Jews do not live in this tension. Only conceptual thinking is in need of a 'leap into faith'.

As to Maimonides's *Thirteen Articles of Faith*, each one beginning with 'Ani ma'amin' translated as 'I believe', two things have to be remembered. First, Maimonides is a scholastic who represents that medievalism which means nothing to us: just as Neo-Thomism has proved unacceptable to a modern generation, Neo-Maimonidism is unacceptable to a modern Jewish generation. Second, we must not forget that Maimonides is a prisoner of the Arabic language. Western scholars of Islam have made it abundantly clear that the Arabic *iman* does not mean belief. It means loyalty. In his *Thirteen Articles* Maimonides does not intend to say each time: 'I believe.' He does not propose to offer a creed. What he does say would read: 'I am a *mumin*, I am a loyal member of my congregation, in which these thirteen points of view are accepted, which can be formulated in different ways at other times and differently by other scholars.'

A student minister, allowed to preach for the first time, said in his sermon: 'If I did not believe in God, I would not stand here.' He deeply moved his Jewish congregation. We speak English and use the word 'believe'. Franz Rosenzweig said, it can be argued that the Jew does not believe in God. An anti-Semite said: 'Never has a Jew really believed in God, never has a Jewish girl really fallen in love.' The difference is clear. Rosenzweig says: The Jew does not *believe* in God. The anti-Semite says: The Jew does not believe in *God*. This may seem theological hairsplitting, but it is necessary. A Jewish State must not force the Israeli citizen into a Pauline belief or into an Islamic concept of law. In the first case the Israeli Jew would be expected to 'leap' into the realm where 'there is no such thing as . . . slave and free-man . . .' (Gal. 3:28). In the second case the Israeli Jew would be denied the distinction between political and religious law. In both cases he would no longer be the free Jew that prophetic Judaism has reared him to be.

SOCIOLOGY OF THE DIASPORA

The Jew belongs to a people which lives dispersed among the nations. State and Church cannot create walls around a people which lives in a diaspora. The State of Israel must not be allowed to create a type of Jew who is predominantly shaped by the influences issuing from the State. A Jew shaped by the State is a Jewish gentile. A dual loyalty can become the problem of the Israeli Jew, proud of and happy with his Jewish State. The late Chief Rabbi Dr Hertz was afraid of this dual loyalty and distinguished between *Ha-tikvah*-Jews and *Sh'ma-Yisrael*-Jews. In our loyalty to the Jewish people in Israel we demand that it should not lose the characteristics acquired in the diaspora. There the Jew is alone with his God, as is the prophet. No creed, no faith in the Pauline sense, binds him to God. God does not let him go, and this makes him a Jew.

Prophetic Judaism is not merely a list of doctrines, summarized as the 'faith of the prophets'. Nor is it the justification of various utopian programmes and of messianic movements in which a generation expresses the hope for its future. The most adequate way of understanding prophetic Judaism is to realize how different the Jew is from all those who live in the closed society of Christianity or Islam. Nowadays the demand to live in an open society has been acknowledged as the condition of freedom. But those who demand an open society as the truly human form of social existence hardly think of the open society in which the Jewish people has lived during its two-thousand-year-old dispersion. The Jewish people has lived under the conditions which a prophet has to endure. Prophetic Judaism is Jewish life shaped not by creed but by the conditions of the diaspora. Jewish life is created by the same force which makes a prophet a prophet. Between God and prophet there is no mediator. Belief has to be upheld, law has to be obeyed, but neither belief nor law is the bond which chains the prophet to God. God takes hold of a man – that is the fate of a prophet. The notion 'prophetic religion' is a contradiction in terms.

God takes hold of the Jew, has him in his grip. This is achieved by Jewish existence in diaspora conditions. The end of the diaspora would be the end of prophetic Judaism. This end would mean the disappearance of the Jew, with his right and his role to stand aloof, to remain separate from the Christian and the Muslim and from all the nations of the world. The joy and the elation which have pervaded all sections of the Jewish people since the establishment of a western Jewish state in the land of the prophets must not blind one to the fact that the Jewish people must remain what it was: a people of the diaspora. Moses could exclaim: 'I wish that all the Lord's people were prophets and that the Lord would confer His spirit on them all!' (Num. 11:29). The prayer of Moses demands a great deal, but not the impossible. Yet it is to expect the impossible to suppose that a Jewish state should become free from the division of its citizens into ruler and ruled, into organizer and organized, into those above and those below. The dichotomy which political existence inflicts on man does not permit him to be a whole man. Christian faith and Muslim law are the historical attempts to solve this dichotomy, which does not arise for the individual Jew in the Jewish diaspora. The Jew speaks to God as a whole man, and this dialogue, as it has lasted in the past millennia, will not break up in the millennia to come. The State of Israel is not outside, but part of, the diaspora. To carry the yoke of the kingdom of God means to carry the yoke of the *galut* (exile). Living under the conditions of the diaspora, the Jew carries the yoke of the kingdom of God. The rise of the State of Israel may wipe away the tears which we shed over the holocaust, but it is not a messianic event. We must distinguish between the true Messiah and the false Messiah. In regard to political messianism we always were and will always remain unbelievers. The difficulties Israel faces are not those of a really sovereign state but those of a diaspora people, sorely dependent on world powers. Israel's present situation is a microcosm of that of mankind.

Jewish life under the conditions of the diaspora rules out both national and denominational unification of the Jewish people. The Zionist acknowledges the impossibility of a national unity of diaspora Jewry and therefore thinks little of the positive role which the diaspora is called upon to fulfil. The ingathering of the exiles, as Jewish nationalists understand it, would be the desired end of the diaspora and would make the Jewish people similar to the gentiles: one nation on one and the same soil. Besides being utopian in a most sterile way, this hope sidesteps the prophetic vision of the One World, of the One Mankind. 'Gather in the exiles' is the messianic prayer for integration of all nations into one mankind under the kingship of God. Men in fear of men, men lacking freedom are the exiles who turn to God with the prayer for the ingathering of the exiles. The exiles crave to return to God's peace, to *shalom*. The Jewish people with its messianic prayer for the redemption of the exiles is like the priest who prays for mankind. In the diaspora we are without the protection of the nation state, we are entirely thrown upon God. He is our shield, or we are lost. This is the prophetic situation of every Jew, be he a simple small shopkeeper or a luminary of science or art. The diaspora makes the Jew. This is how the election of God works.

A denominational unity is no more possible for the Jewish people than national unity. The word 'Judaism' does not denote a denomination as do the words 'Christianity' and 'Islam'. We have already said that a prophetic religion is a contradiction in terms. Only Paul's Christianity and Mohammed's Islam are monotheistic religions. Prophetic Judaism with its very element of prophetic reaction to historic situations is not a religion. Paul and Mohammed are the founders of their respective religions. A prophet is not a founder of a religion. We see Moses as a prophet, and this makes him different from Paul and Mohammed, who must be revered as founders of the two monotheistic religions which have grown out of Jewish life. Within monotheistic civilization Jews move between Christianity and Islam, always scrutinizing them critically, assimilating themselves to them, always seeing them as partners in a world historic dialogue, always seeing them as flesh from their flesh, but never identifying themselves with them.

The role of standing between Christianity and Islam and deciding whether to agree with one or the other has fallen on the Jew. Shall he learn from the Christian creed to emulate the leap into the realm of the spirit, or shall he, like the Muslim, reject it? Shall he follow the method of the Muslim and accept the medium of the law to create a social life which is human and has its character of holiness? A Jewish groping between the Christian and Islamic approach will become evident in the Jewish decision concerning vicarious suffering.

VICARIOUS SUFFERING

Chapter 53 and other texts from the Book of the so-called Second Isaiah preach the message of vicarious suffering. In western Jewish religious thought from Geiger to Baeck the text 'to be a light to the nations' (49:6) was explained as the very contribution rendered to mankind by the Jew. Yet there are second thoughts today after the holocaust, after the third *churban*, during which six million Jews were tortured and murdered. We are now not so sure about the doctrine of vicarious suffering. The Muslim theologian calls vicarious suffering immoral. 'Why should anybody else suffer for me?' he asks and rejects the idea propagated in Christian lands through the symbol of the Cross. Many Christians who were sincerely shocked by the suffering of the Jews during the Nazi persecution appeased their troubled consciences in the end with the pious sigh that Jews had always had to pay the price of vicarious suffering for being the chosen people. This is the point where the Muslim's indictment 'immoral' is right. To make the doctrine of vicarious suffering the excuse for inflicting or ignoring suffering is indeed immoral.

Islam still remembers and reveres the wandering preacher al-Hallaj (Husayn ibn Mansur, 858–922), who died a martyr. In his biography are all the elements which could have made him the Jesus of the Muslim. In him vicarious suffering could have been extolled as necessary for the salvation of man. Islam avoided the temptation. Eventually the execution of al-Hallaj was said never to have taken place, just as the execution of Jesus is denied by Islam. Allah does not need the sacrificial death of man for the sake of the salvation of man. But the stories of the miracles performed by this Persian martyr who announced: 'I am the Truth' ('*ana Haqq*') are still reverently told today.

For the Muslim Jesus is a prophet, and it would be blasphemy for him to believe that God would let his prophet suffer ignominy, torture and death through execution. Surah IV, 157 therefore announces concerning Jesus: 'They did not kill him, they did not crucify him, it was made to appear so to them.' In the Cross, in the doctrine of vicarious suffering Christian and Muslim convictions oppose each other in an irreconcilable way. The Cross reminds man that there is an inevitable tragedy and man owes it to God to remain involved in it. Like the outcome in Greek tragedy, the tragedy on the Cross is inevitable. Islam rejects the belief of the crusaders, of any creative man, that the way to the crucifixion has to be trodden. Invited by the muezzin the Muslim sets out for *falah*, for the good life. In the spirituality of the Christian and in the humaneness of the Muslim, civilization has its two denominations, its two established religions, and both contradict each other. Writers, thinkers, artists, soldiers, all those who give their lives on the altar of history, are the eternal crusaders, looking to the Cross as their archetypal symbol. In obedient resignation to the will of God the Muslim sees the whole world as a mosque and as in no need of redemption. He gathers all the forces of his heart and his mind for prayer. Crusader or worshipper, Christian or Muslim – which is more favourable in the eyes of God? A prophet is needed to answer this question. Jewry, with its prophetic Judaism still alive, is forced to answer, and it is to be hoped that it will answer in the right way. For a thousand years – from the geonic period up to the rise of Zionism – we lived in such a symbiosis with Islam that medieval Christians identified Jews with Muslims. It is owing to the apocalyptic character of our time that we joined the crusaders of our day and fought the Muslim on the battlefield. Our beloved youth who shed their blood in the Six Day War died the death of vicarious suffering. Their vicarious death saved the Israeli *Yishuv* from extinction. We say: 'Glory to the Jewish soldiers of the Six Day War, glory to all those who gave their lives for the State of Israel', and so saying we contradict the Muslim's negative evaluation of vicarious suffering. But does Auschwitz not make us unhesitatingly agree with the Muslim?

65

Is it not 'immoral' to 'explain' Auschwitz with the doctrine of vicarious suffering? This doctrine has for two thousand years been preached by the Cross. Does Auschwitz not make an end to the sermon of the Cross? It does, says Emil Fackenheim in his deeply moving theological reactions to Auschwitz. He also draws a consequence for Jews themselves. Jews have always seen it as their duty to sacrifice their lives for the sanctification of the Holy Name (*kiddush hashem*). After Auschwitz another duty remains uppermost: our continued existence. We have to endure as Jews. If we were to disappear from the stage of history, Hitler would have won.

No less a man than Goethe finds the Cross to be a terrifying symbol, ghastly in its very appearance. In his pedagogical programme for a reformed school he demands that the cross be veiled in order to prevent it from being seen by the young; they should be protected from the trauma which the man cruelly hung on the cross must inflict on their minds. But is not the martyr to be acknowledged in his holy mission for his fellow-man?

Muslim theology makes an important contribution to the dilemma posed by the doctrine of vicarious suffering. The Cross is a sign of victory. It is not that this victory is not credible – the Jew will not doubt the credibility of the idea that the merciful God has the last word. But the Cross stands in the glory of publicity, and in this it does not represent a man who suffers in the anonymity of his own fate. Far away from his fellow man, not recorded by any gospel writer, historian or any justifying authority, man suffers. Job represents the anonymous sufferer. The Cross is a victory sign glorifying vicarious suffering in history. Muslim theology has nothing else to say of the saint than that he was a good man. The Church acknowledges saints only when the *gesta sanctorum*, the deeds of the saints, prove their graduation to sainthood. The Cross is the promise that creative man is lifted up and brought home to his Creator. The Servant of God (Isa. 53) does not merely stand for creative man, he stands for man. The Jew is anonymous man. Behold the Jew. Thus suffers man.

For the pious Christian the Cross is the symbol of martyrdom.

But we must ask whether the killing through burning, torture and sophisticated executions practised in the Middle Ages had its brutalizing cause in the image of the Cross. People came to watch an execution armed with supplies of food and drink. The men with their wives and children watched someone executed on the wheel – a very long-drawn-out process. What steeled the nerves of these people? Was it perhaps the sadistic contemplation which any cross could throughout the years arouse in a primitive mind? In the churches paintings drew attention to the saints with realistic illustrations of the forms of their martyrdom, their execution, showing their mutilation in stages, the ground strewn with severed limbs. An eyewitness tells us how long the strongly built Jan Hus battled with the flames and how hideously he screamed. The screams were ignored by the recorder of the *gesta sanctorum*. Thus rose a generation, which tortured, burned, killed millions of Jews and non-Jews in the Nazi period.

They did so in countries where the Cross was exhibited everywhere. In Poland one could not walk down a country lane without encountering again and again the stern spectacle of the man dying in agony from his cruelly inflicted wounds. In the countryside, where the Nazis built Auschwitz and Treblinka, the Cross was the distinctive characteristic. Vicarious suffering is holy. Cruelty is demonic. The Cross preaches about both. So does the text of Isaiah 53. But the sermon of the Cross turns to the onlooking eye. Chapter 53 in the Book of Isaiah preaches the same sermon, but the cruelty is not visible. The eye is not chaste. It is the lustful eye. The word spoken or read turns to thinking man, feeling with, and responsible for, his fellow man. The lustful eyes of the gentiles gaze at the Cross and reveal what no evangelist had any intention of revealing: the lust of perverted man, inflicting pain on man and enjoying it. The image of the Cross and the Christian imagery of heaven and hell are creations of an imagination which needs purification through analysis. Jews have, in fact mankind has, a vested interest in a revived Christianity. 'Strike the Jew, and you strike man' (Kafka).

The Zionist took a leaf out of the book of the Muslim theologian and cried out: '*Genug gelitten!*' 'We have suffered enough!'

67

The Zionist agrees with the Muslim theologian who says: vicarious suffering is immoral. The Zionist rejects the Christian interpretation of Isaiah 53. But Kafka's religious poetry might teach us that vicarious suffering is there in mankind's history. This Jew, sensing the years of the holocaust to come, describes the lot of such a one 'who bore our sufferings' (Isa. 53:4). He did it in his novel *Die Verwandlung* (*Metamorphosis*). There is nothing of the trappings of the Hellenistic history of the Gospels, there is no Roman cross in Kafka's 'crucifixion' story: Prague at midnight; a dehumanized commercial traveller breathes for the last time, after his thoughts have reverted in love to his family. It is the view of Kafka that somebody must suffer unhappiness, even die, so that others may live and be happy. Of the death of him who represents Isaiah's Servant, Kafka writes: 'He died like a dog.' We can accept Kafka's interpretation of Isaiah 53 even with the experience of the holocaust and ask: Who are the Christ-killers? The answer is clear: The gentiles are the killers.

SOCIAL LEGALITY

Besides the acceptance or rejection of the doctrine of vicarious suffering there is the clash between personal morality and social legality, which divides the Christian from the Muslim. Obedience to the law can be 'the done thing', the thing one does 'because the Joneses do it'. Actions performed in obedience to personal morality rank higher than actions performed in obedience to social legality. This is self-evident to the Christian but the Muslim sees with satisfaction the good end-result achieved through social legality. The Christian does not. The Muslim is human, the Christian strives rigorously for perfection. Christian scrutiny discovers that man guided by social legality lags behind his real moral obligation. Somebody who seems to be 'a good man doing good things' may in fact deceive himself and others by his favourable public appearance. He stands there 'among the righteous' and may be nothing of the kind. Living in harmony with social legality the bourgeois can say: 'I have a clean record.' He and people like him make the city and the suburb a place of law and order even if not a place of saints. This counts for much. Respectability and moral perfection are different from each other but society owes a lot to man sticking to the rules of respectability. 'No cries of distress in our public places' says the Psalmist with satisfaction.

The words of Psalm 144:12–15 are a prayer of thanksgiving coming from the heart of the bourgeois. But they also express *al-falah*, the 'Good' to which the muezzin invites all men in his call from the minaret. Messianic dreams no longer move the heart with restless desire. The world is at peace when families dwell in their homes. In these homes a human, not a spiritual, happiness prevails. Who does not wish to achieve this happiness? The call of the muezzin announces that this happiness exists and is available to all human kind. Nobody needs to be ashamed of longing for this happiness. The words of the Psalm express what man, who is honest with himself, desires:

> Happy are we whose sons in their early prime
> stand like tall towers,
> our daughters like sculptured pillars
> at the corners of a palace.
> Our barns are full and furnish plentiful provision;
> our sheep bear lambs in thousands upon thousands;
> the oxen in our fields are fat and sleek;
> there is no miscarriage or untimely birth,
> no cries of distress in our public places.
> Happy are the people in such case as ours;
> happy the people who have the Lord for their God.

To the Islamic rehabilitation of social legality one has to add the fact that Islam is a religion aiming at the good life. Islamic society purports to be a welfare society. The call of the muezzin from the minaret invites the worshippers to an alert response to *al-falah*: 'Come ye unto the Good.' *Falah* is the state of welfare and prosperity of the people of God, fulfilled in communal existence and realized in social life. The call of the muezzin invites to prayer (*salat*) and to the good life. The Muslim, satisfied with social legality, and the Christian, discovering sin and selfish motives in man, even while he obeys the laws, are radically different from each other. The Muslim will be seen by the Christian as a bourgeois. The Christian is not a bourgeois. The Cross shatters the peace to which the muezzin invites the worshippers. The Cross makes the longing for the good life a treasonable enterprise. Christianity has never come to the defence of the bourgeois. Man living his life according to social legality, and man with a restless conscience about his involvement in the immoral, are two different types of man. In the realm of monotheistic civilization the Muslim can be praised for being human, the Christian for being spiritual. But only the man who is neither Muslim nor Christian can combine Muslim humaneness with Christian spirituality. The Jew is this man. He is a Jew not through the spiritual faith of Paul nor through the law of Mohammed. Neither creed nor law constitutes prophetic Judaism. A Jew need not be expected to be what those giants – the prophets of the Bible – were. A simple Jew speaking of God and seeing his life bound up with God without a 'leap into faith', and without slavery to social legality, is the man guided by prophetic Judaism. There are many doctrines and many laws recorded in Jewish Scriptures which Jews cannot afford to ignore but which they have to re-interpret again and again. But no doctrine, no theory, no creed nor any law makes a Jew what he is as a Jew. He is a Jew by listening and responding to the call of the One God. From state and culture many and various calls come and make their demands on man. They cannot make a Jew – a Jew. There is no 'Jewish' state. There is a state of which Jews are sovereign citizens. There is no 'Jewish' culture, although Jews can be passionately and successfully engaged in culture. What is Jewish is the Jew who hears and understands the message that God is One.

CHRISTIAN AND MUSLIM BEHAVIOUR IN WORSHIP

The next clash between Christianity and Islam which we have

to consider leads us into the field where we watch Christian and Muslim in the way they pray. They do not pray in the same way. The worship of the Muslim is never propped up by culture. Usually we think in this respect of the prohibition of pictures. We face the intensity of Islamic praying when we remember a camel-driver at the time of prayer somewhere where there is no mosque. He has his prayer mat with him and, oblivious of his surroundings, he prays with the prescribed ritualistic movements of his body, lifting his hand, prostrating himself and pronouncing the words which he has learnt to memorize as a child. No silent prayer for him. His lips are continually in motion. The Christian inwardness in prayer would appear to the Muslim as if the worshipper had stopped praying. Can western man learn again to pray in this way? Jews remember the moving lips of their grandfathers. Today they still read the words of their prayer book which run: 'O Lord, open my lips . . .' The Christian failure to face up to Muslim prayer with understanding is obvious: they speak irreverently of the mumbling of prayers. Christian devotion becomes profound when prayers are sung.

The Christian, so the Göttingen theologian Joachim Jeremias alleges, calls God *abba* (Aramaic for 'daddy'). The Christian sees himself as a child of God, the Muslim thinks of himself as a slave of God (*abd*). It would be a great mistake to regard the Muslim as primitive and the singing Christian as superior to him. What we have to acknowledge is the power with which the Muslim can pray. As this power is not with the westerner, he has to bring in art, culture and also creed to substitute for the absence of power and fervour. People who pray are today vastly outnumbered by the scientists and the great number of those influenced by the scientists. The singing worshipper, the worshipper who needs the crutches of culture when approaching God, is on the same level as the scientist. Culture and science are both immanent in the secular sphere. The Muslim with his power of prayer is poised to break through the walls of the secular world. The worshipper with his singing and the scientist with his abstract world will often remain within these walls. *Cave musicam!* Music can become the opium of the cultured. An atheist listening to Bach's *St Matthew Passion* can enjoy this profound work and yet remain within the aesthetic sphere.

In the mosque prayer, it is not creed which is in the foreground. In the Church the creed has a greater importance than prayer. The spirituality of Christian and the robust humanity of Muslim worship represents the two types of worship prevalent in mono-theistic civilization. I have avoided the controversy which dominated Jewish worship during the last century, and I have called the Jewish worshipper a 'book-reading worshipper'. He can, in my experience, combine the power of devotion with an intellectual attitude.

Yet when all is said about the difference between church and mosque service, the two forms of divine service both have their genuine place in monotheistic civilization. A psalm, a hallelujah, sung by congregation or cantor can have the same power which is in the plain-chant of the Muslim and in the words which he utters as if addressing someone directly in front of him. The cultural behaviour in the mosque is different from that in church. The synagogue worshipper cannot but follow sometimes the one, sometimes the other, of the two patterns. The Muslim's worship, built up in an intentionally prosaic approach by spoken words, has its grandeur. But so has the use of the sung word assisted by the organ.

THE JEWISH WORLD DIASPORA

Israel, although part of the Jewish world diaspora and subject to the social and political laws of the rest of the Jewish diaspora, will arrive at its own national, its Israeli, identity. But the other parts of the diaspora have also done this. The American Jewish diaspora and the European one have their own individual, we may even say national, identity. True, the Jewish people every-where look to Israel. A circle has a centre. Is Israel this centre? An ellipse has two foci. Do American and Israeli Jewry provide these two foci? But has not each part of the Jewish world diaspora the right and the need to live according to its particular cultural and social conditions? Uniformity would stifle the creative possibilities which could enrich the global Jewish diaspora in its various parts. What Israel cannot provide, European or American Jewry might. Exuberant hopes concerning an Israeli contribution, pessimism concerning American Jewry and entire neglect of a possible reawakening of European Jewry, will not do. The main fallacy is the assumption that a so-called Jewish culture flowing from Israel to the other parts of the Jewish diaspora would heal the wounds of the post-holocaust Jewish people. To get rid of this fallacy we must come to a true assessment of the creative possibilities of American Jewry, of those of European Jewry, and of the meaning of the concept of Jewish culture.

Ernst Bloch says that European culture can hibernate in America but that it cannot blossom there again. George Steiner is similarly pessimistic. He sees the rise of a 'museum culture' in America. In his T. S. Eliot Memorial Lectures he writes:

> nowhere . . . have the conservation and learned scrutiny of the art or literature of the past been pursued with more generous authority (than in America). American libraries, universities, archives, museums, centres for advanced study, are now the indispensable record and treasure-house of civilisation. It is here that the European artist and scholar must come to see the cherished after-glow of his culture. Though often obsessed with the future, the United States is now the active watchman of the classic past.
>
> It may be that this custodianship relates to a deeply puzzling fact. Creation of absolutely the first rank – in philosophy, in much of literature, in mathematics – continues to occur outside the American milieu. It is at once taken up and intelligently exploited there, but the 'motion of spirit' has taken place elsewhere, amid the enervation of Europe, in the oppressive climate of Russia. There is, in a good deal of American intellectual, artistic production (recent painting may be the challenging exception), a characteristic near-greatness, a strength just below the best. Could it be that the United States is destined to be the 'museum culture'? (Steiner, 1971, p. 86.)

Jewish pessimism is also expressed in the comparison of America with Hellenistic Alexandria. But is not Alexandria the birthplace of Philo, who is not only the 'father' of Christian theology but also a creative influence on Pharisaic Judaism?

73

His method of allegory did so much to prevent Sadducaic biblicism from being accepted by the Pharisaic rabbis. Bloch and Steiner say that no cultural creativity is to be expected from the United States. Even if their lament is true, the question is: what comes after the end of culture? People can live their happy individual lives even after poets and painters have become impotent imitators of a once creative past. Those who make culture an absolute are blind to what is besides culture and beyond culture. The breakdown of culture, the breakdown of creative man, can be the beginning of the flow of contributions coming from man who is not a creator but is, as God's creature, human. Poets, composers, architects may stop finding new ways of expressing themselves. But man outside the circle of aesthetic works has still a wide field to express his humanity in a blissful and a wonderful way. The university may be forced at the end of an age to carry on in old repetitive ways. In the home of man a 'new song' is sung in each generation. A culture may become petrified, but with the birth of her child each mother greets a new day and welcomes what is uniquely new.

Those who pin their hopes for a unified Jewish world diaspora on a Jewish culture should be reminded that culture – the aesthetic component of civilization – is a German concept. Two Germans are responsible for the role of the word culture: Luther and Goethe. Luther never came to terms with a *gnaediger Gott* (a merciful God): It was not the fatherhood of God, but God as holy spirit that made Luther's theology. The Christian believer and the artist both pray: *Veni creator spiritus.* Come Holy Ghost! Belief in culture has its Christian roots. So far Luther. With Goethe the concept of culture dominates the secularized German scene. Goethe formulated: If you have art and science you have religion, if you do not have art and science you need religion. 'Art and science' – culture, for Goethe they are the substitute for religion. With the aim of a 'Jewish culture', Zionists pursue a dated German ideal.

Those who express their exaggerated hopes, and those who give vent to their despair when they view the prospects of culture in our time both make a decisive mistake. They speak – especially in America – of our Jewish-Christian civilization. Both leave out the great contribution of Islam. But can one really suppose that the immense impact of Islam on Europe in the Middle Ages should have disappeared without leaving behind something of its way of life, so different from that of the crusaders, so different from Promethean culture! The word *falah*, the muezzin's invitation to the good life, is the key word indicating what a Jewish-Christian civilization still needs to acquire in order to become a Jewish-Christian-Islamic civilization. It needs true civilization, proper order of human civility. Therefore reference has had to be made in a preceding chapter to the bourgeois. The bourgeois is not respected by the artist. But it is the bourgeois who corrects an inhuman order entirely built up by men outside the family, outside the home and forgoing the happiness available to man. The Hebrew word *baal-habayit* (father of the house) denotes the man who follows the muezzin's call to the good life.

The cultural decline of the Jewish-Christian civilization can – if the muezzin's invitation is accepted – lead to a renaissance of our Jewish-Christian-Islamic civilization. With the integration of what Islam has to give to America and Europe, our civilization becomes the truly monotheistic civilization. Our civilization needs Jew, Christian and Muslim.

There is no need to blow Spengler's trumpet and to despair, as does George Steiner in his T. S. Eliot Memorial Lecture. In his Stephenson Memorial Lecture 'Europe since Hitler', the historian Alan Bullock (1970) reviews the twenty-five years which have passed since 1945 and praises the vitality which Europe has shown in rebuilding the ravages of war. Professor Laqueur too is optimistic about Europe. He writes:

> Not decay but the resilience, the will to survival, that Europe displayed after 1945 constitutes the great novelty, and a source of renewed hope for its future. Far from dying in convulsions as Sartre had predicted, Europe has shown a new vigour which has astonished friends and foes alike. European ideas and techniques have spread to all corners of the earth and European civilisation is still the model for the entire world. The age of European political predominance has ended but no other centre has so far wrenched from

75

Europe the torch of civilisation. In a wider sense the European age has only begun (Laqueur, 1970, p. 403).

The optimism of Laqueur and Bullock is based on sound research. The nineteenth-century concept of 'Jewish culture' confines our hopes for the future entirely to Israel. Understandable as this is, it is not at all in the interest of Israel. It is in her interest that new life should return to the Jewish diaspora: 'You yourselves will see it with your own eyes; you yourselves will say: "The Lord's greatness reaches beyond the realm of Israel"' (Mal. 1:5).

REVELATION

On page 151 of *The Star of Redemption* we read the monumental words: 'The ways of God are different from the ways of man, but the word of God and the word of man are the same. What man hears in his heart as his own human speech is the very word which comes out of God's mouth.' Here is the door leading to Rosenzweig's *Das neue Denken* ('The New Thinking'; see Glatzer, 1953). In the short space of time between 1917 and 1923 Franz Rosenzweig, Martin Buber and the Austrian Ferdinand Ebner experienced, independently of each other, a breakthrough to something radically new in the philosophy of Western thought. Whether Wittgenstein also belongs to this group has still to be considered.

Franz Rosenzweig discovers Speaking Man in contrast to Thinking Man. He says as a Jew what Ebner says as a Christian, quoting St John's words 'The word was God', and what Buber trumpets into the world with the formula 'I – Thou'. The dialogical relationship as an 'I – Thou' relationship was discovered in the terrible experience of World War I. Ebner confessed that when the human person was degraded and cruelly exposed to an 'It', the dignity of man had to be recognized anew and had to be defended. For Rosenzweig, too, the war was the background for this 'New Thinking' which is based on dialogical thinking. As soldiers, Rosenzweig and Ebner were aware of the 'I – It' relationship and therefore longed for the 'I – Thou' relationship which was possible in civic life. Buber's dialogical thinking originated in his opposition to the German school system. In it, the teacher was a kind of sergeant-major and the pupil the recruit. In the German classrooms Buber saw an 'I – It' relationship which had to be redeemed by its transformation into an 'I – Thou' relationship. At this point the difference between teacher and leader has to be carefully watched. The leader does not teach, he fascinates. In the 'I – Thou' relationship the 'I' and the 'Thou' are equals. Where the 'Thou' is enraptured by an 'I', the equality between the 'I' and the 'Thou' vanishes. The inequality of a powerful 'I' and an overwhelmed 'Thou' is the seed of fascism.

The three thinkers – Rosenzweig, Buber and Ebner – saw the end of World War I as the end of feudalism and militarism. They were realistically optimistic about the future. They greeted the rise of democracy by hailing dialectical thinking as the future philosophy. They propagated dialogical thinking as a biblical message long before Vatican II demanded a 'dialogue' with the non-Catholic religions. After long centuries of misunderstanding and the hostility between Christians and Jews and Christians and Muslims, the word 'dialogue' became the key word for the three monotheistic religions and also for the Asian religions.

Rosenzweig's dialogical thinking has follower sin Germany today, especially among Catholic theologians (see Casper, 1967). In the Anglo-American West, Chomsky and those around him went a different way from Rosenzweig, Buber and Ebner. Buber did much to make the West aware of Rosenzweig's linguistic philosophy. It is to be hoped that followers of Wittgenstein will make use of Rosenzweig's new approach which, if accepted, will open up a new chapter in Western philosophy.

In Rosenzweig's *The Star of Redemption*, revelation is understood as a dialogue between God and man and between man and man. Rosenzweig brushed the scholastic interpretation of the word 'revelation' aside, and sees it as the word of the prophet: a word spoken by man, yet being the word of God. After Rosenzweig, the medieval 'two sources' theory – of Maimonides and Thomas Aquinas – is no longer possible. Nor can modern

Orthodoxy enlist help from a neo-Maimonidean theology. Rosenzweig repeated again and again: 'I am a Liberal.' It was of no avail. Orthodox Jews claimed Rosenzweig as their philosopher. In Shakespeare's *Julius Caesar* Cinna cries out: 'I am Cinna the poet, not Cinna the conspirator.' The mob will not listen and attacks him.

Rosenzweig also distinguished between the spoken and the written word. The spoken word addressed to a fellow-man in dialogue mediates revelation. The spoken word is the medium of the prophet. *Nabi* (prophet) means speaker. The written word can lose this prophetical immediacy, as Rosenzweig discovers in his extensive survey of Islam.

> The first word of the revelation to Mohammed says: Read! He is shown the page of a book; it is a book that the archangel brings down to him from heaven in the night of the revelation . . . Islam . . . is a religion of the book from its first moment on; the book is sent down from heaven. Can there be a more thorough renunciation of the concept that God himself 'descends', himself gives himself, surrenders himself to man? He sits enthroned in his heaven of heavens and presents to man – a book (*Star*, p. 166).

It is not only Islam, with its belief in the infallibility of the Koran, which can become a book-religion. Christianity faces the same danger. Thomas Aquinas explains the Bible as the divinely inspired manual about matters not open to human information and reflection. God gave us revelation, he says, and He did so in the Bible. Four centuries after Thomas Aquinas, the following conversation takes place between Christian and Pliable in *The Pilgrim's Progress*:

> Pliable: . . . And do you think that the words of your book are certainly true?
> Christian: . . . Yes, verily; for it was made by Him that cannot lie.

From here we can go on to the comic story of the man who said he would believe that Jonah swallowed the whale, if the Bible said so (see Hodgson, 1968, p. 72). Rabbi Dr Leo Baeck used to address the students who were starting their rabbinical training at the Hochschule as follows: 'The Torah was written just like the works of Goethe and Shakespeare.' We Jews are protected from the danger inherent in the written word through the doctrine of *Torah she-b'al-peh* (oral law), in which the Pharisaic rabbinate retained the living revelation of the spoken word within the written word. This liberation of the human mind is sorely absent in Sadducean Judaism and in modern Orthodoxy. When historical criticism is not applied to the Gospels or to the Torah, Gospels and Torah each become a Koran, a 'good book', a book not intellectually approached but magically endowed with information.

It was the longing of philosophers from Thales to Hegel to reach the transcendent world. This longing must remain unfulfilled, if the philosopher is a monological thinker. Rosenzweig established the philosopher as a speaking thinker, who addresses his fellow-man in a dialogue, and, through his fellow-man, God. The spoken word is immanent in the speaker and transcends him. Immanence and transcendence need no longer be seen as opposites: they are together in speaking man. This dialogue has taken place since Adam; as Rosenzweig says: 'God had no need to wait for Sinai or Golgotha.'

In his book *Das Neue Denken*, published after *The Star of Redemption* (and unfortunately only partly translated into English), Rosenzweig explains:

> It is quite justified that the temples of the gods have crumbled, and their images stand in museums. The part of their service which was governed by prescribed rites may have been nothing but stupendous error, yet the prayers that rose to the gods from a heart in torment, the tears in the eyes of the Carthaginian father offering his son up to Moloch – these cannot have remained unheard and unseen. Did God wait for Mount Sinai or, perhaps, Golgotha? No paths that lead from Sinai and Golgotha are guaranteed to lead to him, but neither can he possibly have failed to come to one who sought him on the trails skirting Olympus. There is no temple built so close to him as to give man reassurance in its closeness, and none is so far from him as to make it too difficult for man's hand to reach. There is no direction from which it would not be possible for him to come, and none from which he must come; no block of wood in which he may not once take up his dwelling, and no psalm of David that will always reach his ear (see 'The New Thinking', in Glatzer, 1953, p. 202).

Rosenzweig emancipated himself – and modern Jewry – from the scholastic understanding of revelation. That God 'came down' (Exod. 19:20) is the great miracle bestowed on man. But we must distinguish between *miraculum* and *spectaculum*. The scholastic *spectaculum* must be demythologized. Rosenzweig has done this. The biblical writer of Exodus 19, although belonging to the group of biblical prophets, is also a great poet. He writes about Mount Sinai covered with smoke, about thunder and lightning, about the people trembling with fear, about God near to them. But already the Midrash, the rabbinical commentary, has demythologized the poetry of Exodus 19 by stressing that only the words 'He came down' are the essence of revelation. Everything else is sermonic addition to the words 'He came down'. 'All that God reveals in revelation is revelation. He reveals nothing but Himself' (Rosenzweig's commentary (1927) to Jehuda ha-Levi, p. 174). Rosenzweig's mother wrote in a letter to him: 'It is rather difficult to believe in the *lieben Gott*' [the German bourgeois 'dear God', a phrase that has nothing at all of the *mysterium tremendum*]. The son's answer shows the religious realism which characterizes his theology. He replies: 'What matters is to have one's five senses open to the world, so open that even *der liebe Gott* may appear as present in it' (see Rosenzweig, E. and Simon, E., 1935, p. 406). I add to this statement of Rosenzweig one of Karl Rahner, S.J.: 'In the world of words there is the word God. This is a miracle established in every man's language. Even an atheist must affirm it. Without this word man would not be man.' God is in the midst of man. Holding fast to this central fact of our life we can say: revelation is our possession. '*Immanu-el*, God is with us', this is the prophetic knowledge called revelation. Man has revelation. It is perverse to deny it and dangerous not to draw consequences from it.

With this emancipation from the scholastic understanding of the event of revelation goes Rosenzweig's warning concerning the word 'religion'. He reminds us that in *The Star of Redemption*, which is a long book, the word 'religion' does not occur, even once (see Rosenzweig, E. (ed.), 1937, p. 374). Furthermore Judaism, prophetic Judaism that is, must not be called a religion.

Fifteen years before Dietrich Bonhoeffer, that modern Christian Saint, coined the term 'religionless Christianity', Rosenzweig reminded Rudolf Hallo in a letter (27 March 1922) that the Jews did not produce a 'religion'. What they achieved in this field – in respect of the Baal and Astarte cults – are mediocre imitations compared with the primeval gigantic religious powers of Sidon and Tyre.

> With us there was always a sober atmosphere. It was, as it still is today, when all the people around us clamour for religion, whereas we, at least the best among us, live our sober lives – certainly with God, but without 'religion'. God did not, after all, create religion, He created the world (Rosenzweig, E. and Simon, E., 1935, p. 430).

With the words 'without religion' Rosenzweig gives expression to the prophetic attitude towards cult. The biblical prophets did not allow cult to become the only medium of man's way to God. This is true. But it is also true that their scepticism concerning cult never amounted to a religious programme without it. To the 'religionless Judaism' which Rosenzweig advocated in an occasional letter, he added his appeal for religious disciplines in his *Star of Redemption* and in the pamphlet *The Builders*. In his dispute with Buber there are a few rituals – Grace after meals, *kiddush* on the eve of Sabbath and festivals – on which Rosenzweig insists. Here Rosenzweig and Buber went different ways.

THE CYCLE OF THE JEWISH YEAR

We have now to consider Rosenzweig's phrase 'anticipation of eternity' (*Star*, p. 328). Rosenzweig wanted to free himself from the nineteenth century which he still found in force around him. People lived after World War I as if this apocalyptic event had never happened. Rosenzweig saw two nineteenth-century movements of a messianic nature that excited people with the promise of a hope fulfilled: socialism and Zionism. He was not tempted to follow either of these two messianic movements. He recognized in the nineteenth century what was also peculiar to the first and second centuries of our era. Hermann Cohen, the head of the philosophical school of Marburg, called Karl Marx a messenger of God, just as Rabbi Akiba had called Bar Kockba the Messiah, and just as Paul turned to Jesus as the Messiah, who had come to fulfil all the hopes of man. Rosenzweig argued as a Jew that every Messiah is a false Messiah as long as history is history. But he respected the false Messiah, as a Messiah progressing towards his cross. Rosenzweig's arguments are those of a (Jewish) non-Christian, not those of an (Islamic) anti-Christian. Rosenzweig was not a sceptic who never allows himself to become committed (see 'The True and the False Messiah', in Glatzer, 1953, p. 350).

Rosenzweig was committed, but not in the way of the nineteenth century or in the way of the centuries of Rabbi Akiba and of Paul. He alone could and did answer the question: Why should we go to synagogue? This question does not ask: What is prayer? The Jewish question 'Why should we go to synagogue?' already has part of the answer implicit in itself. In the synagogue we pray, but not like Christians. They pray as a community of souls. We pray as a community of people.

Rosenzweig discovered – or, better, rediscovered – the eternity present today, he rediscovered the eternal cycle of the Jewish year and therefore the eternity which makes the Jewish people the eternal people. Around us history goes on. The Jewish people, anticipating eternity by standing in the cycle of the Jewish year, anticipating eternity by living from sabbath to sabbath, from festival to festival, no longer changes from one epoch to another. The kingdom of God anticipated as present in the eternity of the Jewish year is no longer a goal to be pursued, it is our home. We live in this home, living through the days and hours which the Jewish calendar uses to direct our lives in our synagogues and within our families. S. R. Hirsch preached a sermon, in which he admonished his congregation with the sentence: The *lu-ach* (the Jewish calendar) is the catechism of the Jew. Rosenzweig followed this simple preacher Hirsch. His description of the Sabbath and festival days is of profound quality. At the time when a Jewish generation had no messianic outlet except socialism and Zionism, he opened in the midst of time a window to eternity.

Rosenzweig served not only his fellow-Jews. He led the way from nineteenth-century secular messianism, from socialism and nationalism, to the non-messianic peace, which was not merely quietism and tranquillity but the peace resting in God. Is there a holy way, holiness towards which we are not driven by messianic fervour? There is, indeed. Is there a non-messianic way of life, which is not a so-called bourgeois way of life? There is. With the words 'anticipation of eternity' Rosenzweig invites his Jewish generation and indeed his whole generation to stand still, to stand in true holiness without a messianic impetus. Why enter the Jewish year or, for that matter, the year regulated by the Christian calendar? The answer is: messianism has spent itself and is no longer true hope but calculating utopianism. To stand still in the eternity anticipated as present is as holy as was the way forward of messianic man. We celebrate redemption by standing still in the worshipping community. The Jewish people has, by being rooted in the cycle of the Jewish calendar, 'suspended for itself the contradiction between creation and revelation. It lives in its own redemption. It has anticipated eternity' (*Star*, p. 328).

The phrase 'anticipation of eternity' is a theological formula and is theologically amplified by Rosenzweig. Yet Rosenzweig is nowhere more successful than in this instance. A generation of intellectuals, humanists and Zionists, had asked the question: Why should we go to synagogue? With this question they meant to say: We are 'good Jews', even if standing outside the synagogue. Those who are socially loyal to the Jewish people and who at the same time forsake the God of the Jewish people think they are entitled to call themselves 'good Jews'. Rosenzweig brought many of them back to the synagogue, to the Jewish year. The Renaissance which Rosenzweig initiated could not unfold itself in its full potentiality owing to the tragedy which continental Jewry suffered with the arrival of Hitler. But a comparison of what Rosenzweig achieved with what Buber created with his romantic interpretation of Hasidism shows the enduring importance of Rosenzweig and the mere temporary

83

success of Buber. Buber also faced the generation of intellectuals, humanists and Zionists who absented themselves from the synagogue. A whole generation seemed to fall away from Jewish life. Buber created for them a romantic island: the world of Hasidism.

THE DAMASCUS ROAD

We have called two quotations from *The Star of Redemption* keys opening the doors which lead to an understanding of Franz Rosenzweig's theology. The first is 'The ways of God are different from the ways of man, but the word of God and the word of man are the same'. The second quotation speaks of 'anticipation of eternity', of 'the Jewish people at its goal', of the suspension of the messianic forward drive. The Jewish people living in the rhythm of the Jewish Year 'has anticipated eternity'. The suspension of messianism makes the heart of man fit to worship God in synagogue, church and mosque. Messianic belief is not replaced by unbelief but postponed with a sober hope for the next chance, when the watchman will herald a new morning after the night.

We now come to a new quotation which reads: The Jew's 'belief is not in something: he is himself the belief' (*Star*, p. 342). This sentence loses its provocative, even paradoxical character when we realize that Rosenzweig repeats here what Geiger and Graetz, in fact the whole rabbinate in nineteenth-century Germany, had stressed before him. They made a distinction between prophetic Judaism and Christian belief. Prophetic Judaism is in no need of dogma and in no need of a fixed Law either. It is different with Christianity and Islam, the first using dogma, the second Law, to establish themselves as distinct denominations. But we had better listen to Rosenzweig himself. He writes:

He (the Jew) is believing with an immediacy which no Christian dogmatist can ever attain for himself. This belief cares little for its dogmatic fixation: it has existence and that is worth more than words. But the world is entitled to words. A belief which seeks to win the world must be belief in something . . . Only he who believes in something can conquer something – namely, what he believes in. And it is exactly so with Christian belief. It is dogmatic in the highest sense, and must be so. It may not dispense with words. On the contrary: it simply cannot have enough of words, it cannot make enough words. It really ought to have a thousand tongues. It ought to speak all languages. For it has to wish that everything would become its own. And so the something in which it believes must be – not a something but everything (*Star*, p. 342).

Rosenzweig is the first, perhaps one can say the only, Jew who bypasses the historical Jesus and turns to the Jesus of the dogma, to Jesus in whom the Christian believes. Rosenzweig does so consciously and logically. How can he do that? He is a Jew firmly rooted in his Judaism. His approach to the Christian faith is phenomenological, descriptive. He asks: What does the Christian believe? What makes a Christian a Christian? Historical research may inform the world that Jesus was an Essene or a Pharisee or, as Joseph Klausner (1922) wrote in his *Jesus of Nazareth*, a nationalist rebelling against Rome. Historical research may still find more details shedding light on the historical Jesus. The historical Jesus, whether or not he is recoverable by the historian, is not the Jesus of the Christian Church. Belief in the Jesus of the Church makes the Christian a Christian. Rosenzweig states the difference between Christian and Jew as the Christian 'believing in something', the Jew 'being himself the belief'. Here he arrives at the difference between belief and prophetic encounter. There is a third possibility besides the Jew's prophetic encounter with God and the Christian belief: the unquestioning obedience of the Muslim. There are three ways to God, the way of the Jew, of the Christian, of the Muslim. Rosenzweig, following Christian theology, did not acknowledge that Islam was, just like Christianity and Judaism, a monotheistic religion.

Acts 9 tells the story of Paul having a vision which changed him as a person. He acquired a faith which he did not have before. This story is, as reliable New Testament scholars assure us, a romance, a fairy tale. It never happened. And yet this story gives us the knowledge of what Paul means when he speaks of faith, of *pistis*, of that belief which makes the Christian a Christian. It is a belief in which a beginning is recorded. It is a belief which erupts in a person as a conversion. Paul becomes what he was not before: he discards what made up his human existence up to now and becomes a 'different man'. He believes. The story of the vision on the road to Damascus is seen as a story of a beginning of the faith in God. Christian belief is momentary beginning. This description of Christian belief leads logically to the statement: the Jew is born a Jew; it is not so with the Christian. 'A Christian is made, not born' (*Star*, p. 396). He is made a Christian in his rebirth. 'He never "is" a Christian, although there is a Christianity. Christianity exists without him. The individual Jew generally lacks that personal vitality which only comes to a man in the second birth . . .' (ibid.).

The Jew feels he is in no need of a 'Damascus road', he need not be 'converted'. He is and has always been at home in his Father's house. The gentiles are in need of conversion. They are the sons of the State and need their Damascus road. The Jews are and must remain the sons of the family. They do not need the Son to bring them into their Father's house; they need no mediator. Herein lies the difference between Jew and Christian.

The Christian approaches only the Son with that familiarity which seems so natural to us in our relationship to God that we for our part can barely conceive of the existence of persons who mistrust this trust. The Christian dares to enter the presence of the Father only through the Son; he believes he can reach the Father only through the Son. If the Son were not a man he would avail nothing to the Christian. He cannot imagine that God himself, the holy God, could so condescend to him as he demands, except by becoming human himself. The inextinguishable segment of paganism which is innermost in every Christian bursts forth here. The pagan wants to be surrounded by human deities; he is not satisfied with being human himself: God too must be human. The vitality which the true God too shares with the gods of the heathen becomes credible to the Christian only if it becomes flesh in a human-divine person of its own. Once this God has become man, the Christian proceeds through life as confidently as we and – unlike us – full of conquering power. For flesh and blood will only be subdued by flesh and blood, and precisely the indicated 'paganism' of the Christian qualifies him to convert pagans (*Star*, p. 350).

A full and harmonious juxtaposition of the historical Jesus and the Jesus of the Christian faith is not possible. The historical Jesus brings a vexing discrepancy before the eyes of the Christians: the Jews. The glory of Jesus in the Jesus of the Christian faith and the Jews whom the Christian meets on the roads of the world – what should the Christian make of this discrepancy? Is it a discrepancy? On the contrary. The Christian is given a proof of the truth of Christianity. Is Jesus a mere idea? It cannot be. The Jews are here in flesh and blood and disprove the suggestion that the Gospel story might be a mere fairy tale. It is history. For this connection with history Christians have to be grateful to the Jews. Jesus was a Jew. The Gospels present Jewish history. The existence of the Jews is historic truth, and in this truth Christian faith participates.

But there is also another point. The reality of the Jews existing in history becomes a stumbling-block for the Christian. The Jew is a foreigner. The Gospel story is a piece of foreign history in the history of every gentile nation. It is annoying and irritating to have a piece of Jewish history grafted onto one's own history. Rosenzweig sees the insoluble contradiction and the indissoluble connection in the two words which make up the contents of the last two thousand years. The two words are: Jew and Jesus. Rosenzweig writes:

The nations have been in a state of inner conflict ever since Christianity with its supernational power came upon them. Ever since then, and everywhere, a Siegfried is at strife with that stranger, the man of the cross, in his very appearance so suspect a character. A Siegfried who, depending on the nation he comes from may be blond and blue-eyed, or dark and small-boned, or brown and dark-eyed, wrestles again and again with this stranger who resists the continued attempts to assimilate him to that nation's own idealization. The Jew alone suffers no conflict between the supreme vision which is placed before his soul and the people among whom his life has placed him. He alone possesses the unity of myth which the nations lost through the influx of Christianity, which they were bound to lose, for their own myth was pagan myth which, by leading them into itself, led them away from God and their neighbour. The Jew's myth, leading him into his people, brings him face to face with God who is also the God of all nations. The Jewish people feels no conflict between what is its very own and what is supreme; the love it has for itself inevitably becomes love for its neighbour (*Star*, p. 329).

CHRISTIAN ANTI-SEMITISM

The two thousand years of Christianity have been two thousand years of hatred for the Jews. This is certainly no generalization. Rosenzweig even speaks of the eternal hatred for the Jew (*Star*, p. 415). If Vatican II really means a change in this, it would be an apocalyptic event bringing blessing not only to the Jews but to the whole of mankind, because both the murderer and his victim are afflicted with the curse which never gives peace to Cain.

Anti-Semitism, although a word coined in Bismarck's Germany, has always been there in the two thousand years of Christianity. We shall not understand anti-Semitism if we approach the evil only sociologically or psychologically. Only a theological approach will help.

'Before God, then, Jew and Christian both labour at the same task. He cannot dispense with either. He has set enmity between the two for all time, and withal has most intimately bound each to each' (*Star*, p. 415). Rosenzweig does not speak here from the approach which the theologian must share with the scientist. He rather speaks with the sorrow which a mournful Psalmist expresses about an unalterable blemish which makes society, even the world, a valley of tears. One point we must accept from Rosenzweig: Anti-Semitism is Christian anti-Semitism.

Western students of Islam have said that Christianity and Islam are irreconcilable opponents; had there been no strong anti-Muslimism in the Middle Ages, there would not have been the many outbursts of anti-Semitism by the Church (see p. 44). Paul and Mohammed are the antipodes within monotheistic civilization. The Catholic theologian Christopher Dawson called Islam the answer to Alexander the Great. The Semitic temperament opposed the polis, opposed Greek civilization. In the same way it can be said, Mohammed is the answer to Paul. Paul's belief, belief constituting Christianity, was replaced by the *sunna*, the *Halachah* of the Muslim.

Mohammed against Paul, the crusader against the Muslim, make up medieval history. This medieval hostility between Christian and Muslim is still alive. One has to understand the hostility between intellectual and bourgeois, the hostility between creative man and man who repudiates creativity for the sake of resigning to the peace of God. That is what the Muslim does. Western man, this Christian Anonymous, has no love left either for the Muslim or for the bourgeois. Western Man calls his civilization Judaeo-Christian and is still in need of discovering the contribution of Islam. It is left to the enemy of Western civilization, the Marxist, to see this contribution. He calls our Western civilization bourgeois civilization.

The Jew, although not involved in the religious war between Muslim and Christian, was seen as identical with the Muslim and was therefore persecuted. We must go back to Rosenzweig's 'God has set enmity between Jew and Christian'. How can the anti-Semite have a place in God's perfect creation? How can He who created the lamb, have created the tiger? God is not responsible for anti-Semitism, the Christian is.

Christian faith is constituted by distinguishing between spiritual and secular. What is the spirit, the *pneuma*? The Christian who believes, believes in the reality of the spirit. The Jew, shaped by the biblical prophets, and therefore deeming possible a direct, unmediated encounter with God, need not contradict the Christian who aims at the inflowing of the spirit into his life and into his Church. The Muslim does. He will not try to understand what the Christian means by belief, with its power of converting man to the spiritual existence achieved in his rebirth. (We have explained what the Muslim understands as belief which he calls *iman*. *Pistis* and *iman* never mean the same, although the westerner translates both by 'belief'.) The Jew stands between Christian and Muslim, understanding both, identifying himself with neither. What the Jew will not accept is the exclusion of the distinction between holy and profane, between holy and human. The Jew objects to the assumption that only the distinction between spiritual and secular constitutes man's life with God. The direct unmediated encounter with God constitutes Jewish life, unquestioning obedience constitutes that of the Muslim, and 'the Damascus road' constitutes Christian life.

In his correspondence with his cousin Eugen Rosenstock, baptized into Christianity as a child by his parents, Rosenzweig argues about the reason for Christian anti-Semitism. Rosenzweig reminded his cousin of the Persian king Xerxes, whose servant, standing behind him at table, said: 'Master, remember the Athenians!' So far the story of Herodotus. But Rosenzweig changed the words of the servant. He writes to Rosenstock on 7 November 1916, that is seven years before he published *The Star of Redemption*: '*Despota, memneso to eschaton* (Master, remember what is absolute)' (Rosenstock, 1969, p. 135). To comment on Rosenzweig's *eschaton*: Remember to whom we turn, when we say: 'Hear, O Israel, The Lord is our God, the Lord is One!' No appeasing apologetics will eradicate the tension between Jew and Christian. The Christian reacts to the Jew with 'enmity'. The translator of the *Star* should have used the word 'hostility', as the word in the German original is *Feindschaft*. It is not enough to speak only of animosity. Here is that enmity which divides Cain and Abel. But why speak only of the Christian hatred for the Jew? The same Christian hatred is also directed against the Muslim. The crusader does not distinguish between Jew and Muslim. Both Jew and Muslim offend the Christian with their denial of the reality of the spirit. The Muslim decidedly does.

With the Jew it is different. He by-passes the Christian doctrine of the Holy Spirit. The Jew need not outrightly deny the existence of the spirit, but will acknowledge it only as an aesthetic category, creative man is driven by the spirit. The prophetic attitude, never developing into an established religion, is critical of, but never aggressive towards, the existence of another established religion. Between Christianity and Islam, between Paul and Mohammed, enmity cannot but persist. But Christian and Jew are not irreconcilable. The Jew will only protest where the spirit becomes the enemy of reality. Reality is God-created reality. The Christian

Church is the monument of the spirit. As people pray to God in church, the Jew will acknowledge the church, as he acknowledges the mosque; but he will not see the spirit as capable of creating a Christian institution with the right of denying that there is 'salvation outside the Church'. The spirit, the Jew contends, is the spirit of man. To this the Christian will respond with anti-Semitism.

The Jew must carry the kingdom of God and suffer anti-Semitism. He must say 'No' to all false absolutes. He must do so not only in the case of the Church but also in the political field. The flag of the State is the most solemn symbol of Western man. Where the flag of the State is itself a kind of sacrament, the Jew says 'No'.

Medieval Islamic society tolerated Jews, Christian society was unable to do so. Christian doctrine according to Romans 11 saw Jews as part of the Christian commonwealth only when all the gentiles had become Christians: before this apocalyptic date 'they are treated as God's enemies' (Rom. 11:26, 28). In Islam, on the other hand, the Jews were *dhimmis*, 'the free non-Muslim subjects of a Muslim government, who pay a poll-tax for which the Muslims are responsible for their security and freedom and toleration' (*Arabic-English Lexicon*, 1863, I, part 3). However remote Islamic tolerance may have been in individual cases from what the liberal State calls tolerance, it was more than the Pauline world granted to Jews. Romans 10 and 11 read like a truly edifying sermon and cannot but be read in this way by Jews looking for an end of the 'enmity between Jew and Christian'. But Paul's admittedly sincere remark 'I am an Israelite myself, of the stock of Abraham, of the tribe of Benjamin' in practice means no more than the anti-Semite's assurance: 'Some of my best friends are Jews.' Much more thinking has to be done by the Christian anti-Semite to purify the world by fighting anti-Semitism.

JEWISH POLITICAL THEOLOGY

Franz Rosenzweig sees the eternity of the Jewish people as guaranteed in the fact that it is a 'community based on common blood'

(*Star*, p. 299). 'Blessed art Thou . . . who hast planted everlasting life in our midst.' There is only one community in which the sequence of everlasting life goes from grandfather to grandson. In a play of words which cannot be translated into English – *zeugen* means both to testify and to reproduce – Rosenzweig states: 'The Jew, engendered a Jew, attests his belief by continuing to procreate the Jewish people' (*Star*, p. 342). Again and again Rosenzweig speaks in his *Star of Redemption* of the 'physical onward flow of the one blood bearing witness to the ancestor in the engendered grandson'.

Needless to say, Rosenzweig is not a racialist, however baffling his emphasis on the term 'the one blood' may be to his reader. Rosenzweig wrote his *Star of Redemption* in the years 1917–23. At that time he had no need to guard his pen against the racialist ideology which had not yet raised its ugly head in Germany. In racialism blood is mystically endowed with something which makes the blood of one race distinct from the blood of another race. Rosenzweig uses the word 'blood' in the sense of the biblical term 'flesh and blood'. 'Generations' (Hebrew *toldot*) or 'children's children' are terms that are relevant to Rosenzweig's concept of common blood. The phrase 'children's children', denoting eternity, never occurs in the New Testament. In the Old Testament it is to be found in numerous places. Man as the creature of God is flesh and blood. All men are equal in that they are flesh and blood. As human beings they all have the same blood in their veins. They are different in their political status and through their political life. It is not a political distinction, or a cultural or a spiritual one, which makes the *am ehad*, 'the only one people', what it is. Rosenzweig turns to the Jewish people with the command of Ezekiel 'In your blood live!' (16:6). When the Jewish people experienced life under the conditions of the diaspora for the first time, Ezekiel warned the exiles not to turn to the surrounding religions, in which man sacrificed and transcended his human existence. Rosenzweig and Ezekiel say one and the same thing to the Jew: 'Be human; you need not search for God in a spiritual beyond; as a human being you have God in your "blood".'

In a Jewish political theology attention is focused on the aim to preserve the whole man: the antithesis 'spiritual – secular' should not affect the Jew. But in the Christian political and spiritual situation, political ideology permits, encourages and even commands man to cease to be a whole man.

Only the whole man is truly human. Kafka and Nietzsche saw the predicament in which the Christian gives up the humanity of the whole man. Kafka speaks of 'Christian coldness'. There is a moving example of this in Graham Greene's *The Power and the Glory*: a Roman Catholic priest who has married and begotten a child under the threat of Communist persecution, meets this child when he is once more a priest. 'Why can I not have a father like the other children?' asks the child. The father remains faithful to his spiritual situation and turns away from his little daughter – a moving illustration indeed of 'Christian coldness'. And Nietzsche? He is a true Christian with his heroic-cruel maxim: 'Man is something that must be surpassed.' Ezekiel and Franz Rosenzweig use the word 'blood' to affirm the non-spiritual but truly human status of being man, whole man, also in his encounter with God. Rosenzweig gives the following explanation: 'We cling to our creatureliness. We do not gladly relinquish it' (*Star*, p. 416). Although Judaism is not a proselytizing religion, it can welcome the proselyte. Jew and Jewish proselyte have in common their 'blood', their 'creatureliness'. What the proselyte who enters the Jewish fold should leave behind, is his political and cultural past. His 'blood' is not an obstacle. Maimonides advised a proselyte who left Islam and became a Jew to pray without hesitation with the worshipping Jewish congregations: 'Our God and God of our *fathers*'.

As a community of common blood the Jewish people is not constituted in the same way as the polis. The Jewish people is made up of families, the polis of citizens. What connects Jew with Jew is in the last analysis not citizenship. The polis can become a church and can thus connect Christian with Christian spiritually. In the Christian Church all are 'brothers'. Anyone who cannot be a 'brother' cannot be a Christian. But the connection between Jew and Jew is not of a spiritual kind. The Jewish people 'does not have to hire the services of the spirit; the natural propagation of the body guarantees it eternity' (*Star*, p. 299). But we must not rush to the conclusion that Rosenzweig regards Jewish life as not fit to exist in the polis. We must carefully watch the difference between the Jewish people as a community of common blood and the rational, the political and the spiritual world in which the man of the polis, the citizen, or for that matter the man of the church, the Christian, lives.

What is, after all, the polis? What is the forum, the *agora* of the Graeco-Roman city which still exists where the state dominates our lives? The forum is an empty space. The homes of the families surround it. In these homes the families, men, women and children live; here they have their meals, sleep, spend their days and nights. The forum is the place only of the men. There they consider and decide upon communal affairs. As an empty space not destined for habitation the forum is a nothing, as the Spanish philosopher Ortega y Gasset emphasizes. He also says that the discovery of the empty space which gives the polis its character is more important than the discovery of that space which goes back to Einstein. The empty space sucks the very possibility of its existence from the surrounding human unit. Still, one must repeat quite emphatically, the Jew can live as a Jew in the realm of the polis. Our Jewish State can, but need not, destroy our Jewish existence as members of the *am ehad*, of the 'only one people', different from all nations. But a grave challenge exists and has to be faced. A mere religious negation of the State will not do for us Jews. The Church is the negation of the State, spiritual order is the negation of political order. Our Jewish State must not be exalted to a Church, our community of common blood must not be spiritualized. The same blood, the blood of fathers alive in the children, not the spirit, must unite the Jewish people. To solve the task we must first of all remain aware of the new situation. In the Middle Ages the juxtaposition of synagogue and church exercised Jewish thinkers and Christian schoolmen alike. Today it is not these two opposites which are under discussion, but three entities: *am ehad* – polis – church. There is even a fourth social unit: the religious denomination which comes into being where political Law and religious Law are seen as identical, of which Islam is the classic example.

The Jew is a Western man. He carries the heritage of the Graeco-Roman world. As a Western man he is a man of the polis, a man of the *urbs*, a man of the city: humane, urbane. The difference between the man of the city and the man of the field is decisive in the history of man, as Ortega y Gasset points out. He wrote his book *The Revolt of the Masses* in the thirties, that is to say later than Rosenzweig wrote his *Star of Redemption*. Both authors are independent of each other. But they have identical views with regard to the polis, and Ortega y Gasset can usefully be employed as a commentator on Rosenzweig. The Spanish philosopher writes:

> The man of the fields is still a sort of vegetable. His existence, all that he feels, thinks, wishes for preserves the listless drowsiness in which the plant lives. The great civilizations of Asia and Africa were, from this point of view, huge anthropomorphic vegetations. But the Graeco-Roman decides to separate himself from the fields, from 'Nature', from the geo-botanic cosmos... (The *polis*, the city is) the negation of the fields... (In it) man frees himself from the community of the plant and the animal... Hence Socrates, the great townsman, quintessence of the spirit of the *polis*, can say: 'I have nothing to do with the trees of the field, I have to do only with the man of the city'. What has ever been known of this by the Hindu, the Persian, the Chinese or the Egyptian?... (The) struggle between these two spaces: between the rational city and the vegetable country, between the lawgiver and the husbandman, between *jus* and *rus*, was won in the West after Alexander and Caesar by the *polis* (Ortega y Gasset, 1951, p. 116).

The biblical prophets regarded the value of the city in the same positive way as did the men of Graeco-Roman antiquity: when the Rehabites argued that the God of the fathers was a God of the desert, Hosea protested: It is the God of the fathers who in the city showered his gifts on Israel and 'gave her corn, new wine, and oil...' and 'lavished upon her silver and gold...' (2:8). But the entry of the Jew into the polis is a step leading into an abstract world, the world of administrators, colonels and generals. Their logistics dictate to the polis. This world can be

95

redeemed – by the Christian Church. The polis can be transformed into a church but not into that community which the 'only one people' represents.

The polis was both State and Church in the pagan world, as Rosenzweig points out (*Star*, p. 352). The State of Israel must never be exalted to such a lofty degree that holiness is ascribed to it. In the Christian world, however, the dictum 'Render to Caesar what is Caesar's' was as important as 'Render to God what is God's'. This dualism God – Caesar gives Caesar the same due as God. The Jew must never solve this dualism in the Christian way. The State of Israel must never achieve the status which a Church assumes. A 'Jewish' polis is unthinkable. But the Jew can reside in the polis, serve its requirements, accept its ways, obey its orders and still remain a Jew. The *K'nesset Yisrael*, the 'House of Israel', is never a polis and is never what the Church is. 'House of Israel' and State of Israel remain distinct from each other. In the Church political concerns are transfigured into spiritual ones. In the *am ehad*, the 'only one people', there are neither political nor spiritual elements. Rosenzweig, it can be said here, uses the term 'the only one people' in preference to 'chosen people'. The gentile nations, all human beings, are chosen, and have free access to God. Jews may say: 'Thou hast chosen us from all peoples', but this is only half the statement. We add at once: '. . . and hast given us the Torah'.

In the chapter 'State and Church' Rosenzweig writes: 'For the Jew, the world is full of smooth transitions from "this world" to the "world to come" and back; for the Christian, it is organized into the great dualism of state and Church' (*Star*, p. 352). This great dualism must not penetrate Jewish life. Jewish life must not be split into a secular and a spiritual sector. We live in the diaspora and in the State of Israel, and thus we become citizens. But we are not transformed into a secular type of man, nor do we, when rooted in the life of the *am ehad*, the 'only one nation', change into a type of man living a spiritual existence. A constant 'transition' from the political existence of the Jew to his non-political existence and back is both possible and necessary.

We must still see ourselves as exiles. As citizens of the State of

Israel and as citizens of any state of our diaspora we have not arrived in the Holy Land. We are still praying: 'Next year in Jerusalem.' We are always in 'transition' from the polis to our 'dwelling alone' and back. We look at ourselves and our fellow-citizens in the State of Israel and everywhere else and pray 'Gather our exiles'. The *galut* has nothing to do with geography. *Galut*, exile, is the pre-messianic situation of the Jewish people and of mankind.

Can the post-Emancipation Jew still retain his non-political existence? We have been emancipated from the Middle Ages. In the Middle Ages the Jew lived without interest in what was going on in the world around him. Rosenzweig describes the pre-Emancipation Jew as a knight, *striding through history without a sideward glance* (as I prefer to translate the sentence). The post-Emancipation Jew, on the other hand, is involved and engaged in the political life around him. Yet the *am ehad*, the only one people, must 'dwell alone'. With his rootedness in the *am ehad*, with his rootedness in the flow of the one blood from ancestor to children's children, with his rootedness in this truly private realm, there is no difference between the pre- and the post-Emancipation Jew. Rooted in his private realm, man can meet God. It is the prophetic meeting in which man speaks to God 'face to face'.

Rosenzweig points out that the nation states rebel against the universalism of the Christian Empire, of the Holy Roman *Reich*. (In the same way Islam is a rebel protesting against the spirituality of the Christian Church.) During his student years Rosenzweig was involved in the controversy between Zionism and Liberalism. In sermons given in synagogues these hotly contested problems were taken up. There was one set of rabbis who stressed universalism, another who preached Jewish nationalism or emphasized at least the closed society of one's own denomination. It was a controversy between Christian spirituality and the Islamic concept of terrestrial holiness, a controversy between Church and State fought out in the pulpits of the synagogue. Only Franz Rosenzweig tackled the real issue of the controversy by confronting the Jewish people with the original, i.e. Graeco-Roman, understanding of the polis. In this way, he, the non-Zionist, eventually arrived at a reconciliation with Zionism by pointing to the constant possibility of 'transitions' from the political to Jewish existence and back.

Rosenzweig realized that the German Zionists around him did not really understand the tragic world into which the state leads man. They only knew the liberal state. In his extensive biography of Buber, Hans Kohn (1961, p. 170) quotes a letter from Buber to Stefan Zweig (in 1918): 'Of a Jewish State with cannons, flags and medals I know nothing, not even in a dream' (see pp. 9–10). Rosenzweig showed the stern reality which the generation of Buber did not grasp. Ben Gurion did. He willed the confrontation with the British, while Weitzmann wanted to avoid it. The British with their knowledge, where liberalism ceases to function, forced Ben Gurion to do as the gentiles do: to fight. The Jewish State was born, because Jews did what they had not done for two thousand years: they wielded the sword. In a world in which Christianity and liberalism were dead and in which the gods of the polis alone mercilessly watched the tragedy of man, no other way was open to the Jews. To say that Rosenzweig was the only Jew who saw what was coming, a quarter of a century before the establishment of the State of Israel, is certainly saying too much. But what can be said is this: all the elements which led to the future, still far off from Rosenzweig's peaceful Frankfurt, were clearly recognized by him. He writes:

> Thus war and revolution is the only reality known to the state; it would cease to be a state at the moment where neither the one nor the other were to take place – even if it be only in the form of a thought of war or revolution. The state can at no moment lay down the sword. It must brandish it again at every moment in order to cut the Gordian knot... (the) contradiction between past and future.... (But to stem the flow of continual change) the state ... introduces standstills, stations, epochs ... (The state) introduces them through its martial spell which makes the sun of time stand still until on any given day 'the people shall have prevailed over its enemies' (*Star*, pp. 333–4).

These epochs within history last as long as they last. Their will to last for eternity is futile. The state can only create a 'sham eternity', as Rosenzweig says. But there is true eternity, the eternity of the Jewish people, of the *am ehad*, of the only one people.

> Therefore the true eternity of the eternal people must always be alien and vexing to the state, and to the history of the world. In the epochs of world history the state wields its sharp sword and carves hours of eternity in the bark of the growing tree of life, while the eternal people, untroubled and untouched, year after year adds ring upon ring to the stem of its eternal life. The power of world history breaks against this quiet life which looks neither right nor left . . . Force may coerce the 'newest' into an identification with the 'final', to make it appear the very newest eternity indeed. But that is not like the bond which obtains between the latest grandson and the earliest forebear. Over and over, our existence sets before the eyes of the nations this true eternity of life, this turning of the hearts of the fathers to their children: wordless evidence which gives the lie to the worldly and all-too-worldly sham eternity of the historical moments of the nations, moments expressed in the destiny of the states (*Star*, pp. 334–5).

Ezekiel's 'in thy blood live!' and Franz Rosenzweig's continuous reminder of the Jewish people as a community of blood point to the family. The family, not the state, builds the House of Israel. We must take care that state, culture, nationhood do not become the stumbling-block for the post-Emancipation Jew.

The Christian yearns for spiritual holiness, the Muslim for terrestrial holiness. In the family both spiritual and terrestrial holiness nestle together. The Jewish people is a human bond, human and in that non-political. Rooted in the family the Jew is, even as a citizen, not a 'political animal', but man as God created him in His own image. In the family there lives the bliss granted to man by God who sent Abraham home, a happy father with his son Isaac alive.* In the polis the noble tragedy of *dulce et decorum est pro patria mori* gives dignity to the sons defending their kith and kin with the sword.

In a letter to Pfarrer Hans Ehrenberg (15 May 1927) Franz Rosenzweig summarized his views about the state:

---

* About the Binding of Isaac in Judaism, Christianity and Islam, see Maybaum (1969).

The first great messianic movement in Judaism (if I exclude the return from the Babylonian exile), the Bar Kokhba movement under Hadrian, which in its outer manifestations was the greatest of all, was purely political, even purely military so far as the person of its leader was concerned. And yet Rabbi Akiba, the greatest *homo religiosus* of the Judaism of the Pharisaic centuries, joined it, declared Bar Kokhba to be the Messiah, and suffered martyrdom for his faith.

From this alone you must realize that we cannot work with concepts exclusively. We must look at the person, at persons.

The prophets observed an objective critical attitude toward their own state, the Pharisees toward the states of the Diaspora. In both cases it was really objectivity, not negation ... (Rosenzweig, E. and Simon, E., 1935).

By pointing to the criticism of the state by prophets and Pharisees Rosenzweig warned his generation not to identify this criticism with cosmopolitanism. The prophets and the Pharisees were not cosmopolitans, they were revolutionary critics of their own State.

Rosenzweig had a success of historic importance: he made non-Zionists work with Zionists. He remained a non-Zionist. He believed in the possibility of Jewish life under the conditions of the diaspora. But the non-Zionist Rosenzweig could write in an often-quoted letter to the liberal Rabbi Bruno Jacob: 'there are better Jews among the Zionists than among us.' This letter is dated 17 May 1927. We write in 1972. It would be foolish to base any generalization on Rosenzweig's warm appreciation of the Zionists around him. The 'better Jews' are there where there is readiness for sacrifice, hope and faith. Let us hope that they are numerous in Israel and in the diaspora.

Yet a Jewish State is unable to preserve Jews as 'the merciful children of merciful ancestors, full of kindness as their ancestors were', as they have been throughout the ages. A state cannot remain the one-class society in which the Jewish people has always lived. A state cannot be a group of families. A state is not a tribe. A state consists of citizens who are divided through the different functions which have to be performed. A sergeant-major may be a friendly chap in private life, but when he yells his commands to his platoon he represents the Caesar whom the citizen has to obey, as he has to obey God. With these two classes, the one commanding, the other obeying, the Jewish one-class community cannot be upheld. Gideon's 'I will not rule over you, neither shall my son rule over you', this charter of religious egalitarianism, is out of place in the state. The 'Hear, O Israel' and the national anthem both uplift the mind in religious devotion, but each in a different way. Paul left Judaism and harmonized the polis and the Church at the price of the dualism between secular and spiritual, between body and soul. Jews have never accepted this dualism. But a Jewish State creates the Jewish citizen's dilemma, and he can solve it if he accepts all the consequences of the dualism taught by Paul. The 'merciful children of merciful ancestors' will, as citizens, become merciful – in the spirit. Rosenzweig was perplexed because he visualized a generation serving a Jewish State implicated in problems for which Christian, not Jewish, solutions can be offered. Christian and Muslim have each a different way of converting the polis. The Christian spiritualizes the polis into a church, the Muslim assimilates the state to a religious denomination by identifying political with religious law. A Jewish cooperation with the state is still possible. But it is the cooperation of the outsider. The commandment 'Love your neighbour as yourself' does not constitute a social unit but remains the bond between two persons only: the lover and the loved. But this non-political bond between two persons, multiplied in groups, can penetrate the state and change it, as leaven changes the dough.

The state can make Jews into Jewish gentiles. Their political status of cooperating outsiders prevents this. To be an outsider as an Israeli citizen-soldier need not, indeed must not, mean non-commitment to the sacrifices which the state demands. Zionists accept the noble values which we accepted in the past in the Hellenistic chapter of Jewish history and which today have their renaissance in Israel. The Jew as non-Zionist, cooperating with the Zionist, is fully justified in rejecting the replacement of Jewish values by the Greek values of military valour. His cooperation can be fully upheld but must needs be that of the outsider. The Jew among the gentiles is an outsider. Fate forced us to become Israeli gentiles. *En b'rera.* 'We had no choice.' But Judaism must not change. As outsiders in our Zionist era, upholding Jewish values we can remain 'the merciful children of merciful ancestors'.

The rightful place of the non-Zionist Jew in the Jewish people was discussed by Leo Baeck and his students at the Hochschule, at the time when Weitzmann established the Jewish Agency in which Zionists and non-Zionists worked harmoniously together. Dr Baeck gave his whole-hearted support to Weitzmann's plan and made a success of it in Germany. German Jewry found its way to the Jewish Agency earlier than American Jewry.

Dr Baeck – like Rosenzweig (*Star*, pp. 364, 369) – emphasized that the Jewish calendar is fixed and cannot be supplemented by new festive days. This is done by the gentiles who commemorate days conditioned by history, days celebrated in rejoicing by one generation and forgotten by the next. The Jewish calendar does not point to history but to deliverance from history. The exceptions are Hanukkah, Purim, and the Ninth of Av. They record historical events and are in consequence not mentioned in the Torah. The book which records Jewish history is the Haggadah (the story of the Exodus from Egypt), 'the story' pure and simple, 'the' Haggadah among all the countless haggadahs (*Star*, p. 364), telling us the glad tidings of deliverance from history.

Revelation as an event in history is recorded in the Christian, not in the Jewish, calendar. Revelation is viewed by the Jew as within creation. As pointed out above (p. 80), there is not even a word for revelation in biblical Hebrew. Creation, described as 'good', expresses all the glories of revelation. The Christian calendar tells a different story. It records a revelation in the midst of history. In the year One, in the country of Palestine, revelation happened. To the Christian, revelation is a historical date. Let us remember the words and the tune of 'Silent Night, holy night'! This is the Christmas message of Pauline Christianity. It is understood by the simple and by the wise. But the Jew regards this carol only as a lovely, pious tune. In the national festivals celebrated by the gentiles the miracle of Christmas, in which the Christian rejoices, repeats itself. We Jews now celebrate *Yom Atzmaut* (Independence Day) and *Yom Yerushalayim* (Day of the liberation of Jerusalem) and we shall – let us hope – celebrate future dates in the national history of Israel. Does this mean that the Christmas spirit now influences Jewish thinking? It could, but it must not happen. The Jew understands Christmas, and the Christian understands the Jewish Sabbath, the 'memorial of the creation'. Yet this Jewish-Christian understanding must not end up in a syncretism in which the Jew is not a Jew and the Christian is not a Christian. Our minds and hearts must turn to the Lord of creation. He and not the many lords, His eternal redemption and not the great days of history, make the worship which the Jewish calendar regulates into Jewish worship.

To the unchanging calendar of the Jewish year corresponds the unchanging status of the Jewish people, different from the gentiles who are engaged in and committed to the changes of national history. In the above-mentioned discussion concerning the Jewish Agency, Dr Baeck said – entirely in the spirit of *The Star of Redemption*: The nations of the world, the gentiles, need a 'reserve-force', not to be consumed by history. The non-Zionist Jewish people is here to help the Zionist fellow-Jew and mankind.

With the clarity of the converted, the Christian anti-Semite Eugen Rosenstock, a cousin of Franz Rosenzweig, sees the situation of the Jew who stands outside history, but is helpfully devoted to the gentiles in their involvement in their national history. On 30 October 1916 Rosenstock wrote to Rosenzweig (both were soldiers in uniform at the time): 'The Jew dies for no fatherland and for no mission' (Rosenzweig, E. and Simon, E., 1935, p. 682). The answer in Kafka's style would be: You are right, on the condition that you are wrong. Rosenzweig's answer, borne out by the whole content of *The Star of Redemption*, could be formulated in this way: the Jew dies not merely for one particular fatherland, for one particular mission. He dies for many a fatherland, for the various particular missions surging up in the conflicts of history. The mission of the Jew, for which he suffers and dies on many battlefields, is only one: the mission to serve man.

THE DOCTRINE OF THE TRINITY

The Hellenistic world, the West, responded to the biblical 'God is One' with the doctrine of the Trinity. To Jews this doctrine is, according to Samuel Sandmel (1965, p. 44) 'inherently incomprehensible'. But the philosophy of Plato or of Kant may also be incomprehensible to many Jews. The doctrine of the Trinity, like the philosophy of Plato and Kant, has to be studied by Jewish scholars. If the doctrine of the Trinity – God, history and the human mind – is studied, the Jewish and the Christian scholar will give different answers. The formula Father, Son and Holy Ghost, regarded by the devout medieval Christian as denoting an inexplicable mystery, has an earlier history, in which the Fathers of the early Church were not merely devout believers, but proved to be thinkers engaged in a gigantic mental struggle. The philosophy within the doctrine of the Trinity is, like a Gothic cathedral, an admirable monument of medieval piety.

The doctrine of the Trinity established that the God, whom Christians address in The Lord's Prayer, is the God of Genesis 1 and 2, the God who created the world. The doctrine of the Trinity established that the God who spoke (and is still speaking) through the prophets is the same God whom Christians hear speak in the Gospels. In so doing, the doctrine of the Trinity rejected the heresy of the Gnostics who contended that the 'old' God no longer reigned in the New Era. The Gnostic Marcion spoke of the 'unknown God' to whom a Greek arriving in an alien country would erect an altar as the true God. The Gnostics did not acknowledge the God of the Old Testament, who was God the Creator. The doctrine of the Trinity, rejecting the various forms of Gnostic heresy, ensured that the Christians, like the Jews, glorified God as benevolent Creator. The doctrine of the Trinity identified 'the Logos who was God' as the Creator of the world. But besides the God-created world, there is history, which is the place of the creations of man. Hellenistic man could still marvel at the impressive achievements of the men of antiquity in literature, art and statecraft. They were acknowledged as the work of the Logos. The doctrine of the Trinity prevented a heresy which would have by-passed the Creator-God of the Jews and worshipped the Logos instead. The Old Testament was not taken out of the canon of 'sacred books'; it was taught that the New Testament is not a substitute for, but an addition to, the Old Testament, which had become necessary through the impact of the surrounding Hellenistic civilization. The dogma of the Trinity emphasized that the New Testament did not bring a new revelation, but one implicit in the old revelation.

The doctrine of the Trinity preserved monotheistic faith against heresies which lapsed back into polytheism, seeing Christ in competition with, but on the same level as, the gods of Olympus. The doctrine of the Trinity preserved Jewish monotheism in the midst of Hellenistic civilization.

Christians adhere to the liturgical formula 'Father, Son and Holy Spirit'. Jews and Muslims decline to accept this formula. Jews have known Christians for nearly two thousand years; and Muslims have known them for fourteen hundred years. During all that time, up to the nineteenth century and up to Hermann Cohen and Franz Rosenzweig, no attempt has been made, either by Jews or by Muslims, to elucidate the doctrine of the Trinity for non-Christians. A belief in the mystery of the Trinity dominates the Pauline centuries, usually called the Middle Ages. A mystery apprehended through faith alone is inaccessible to doctrinal comprehension. A philosophico-theological understanding of the Trinity, on the other hand, brings the Pauline centuries to an end and initiates a new era for Jew, Christian and Muslim. A trialogue between the three is possible when the doctrine of the Trinity, properly analysed, ceases to be the issue which disrupts the union of the three different but equally monotheistic faiths. When the Sphinx is made to yield her mystery and is addressed by her name, no longer veiled in secrecy, she sinks to the bottom of the sea, and time can flow forward to a new era.

The clause 'through Jesus Christ our Lord' must not be seen as a spoken talisman, which the worshipper includes in prayer and devotion. This clause and the word 'name' (Hebrew *shem*), in biblical sentences, have similar functions. Psalm 115:1 reads:

'Not to us, O Lord, not to us but to thy name ascribe the glory.' The Jew knows of 'the holy name' (*shem hakodesh*), which only the High Priest in the Temple was allowed to utter on the Day of Atonement. 'The holy name', which we do not pronounce, expresses God's whole nature. But there are 'a thousand names of God', to use a phrase of the Muslim, in which prophets, priests and laymen express His inexhaustible nature. God is our Father, our King, our Shepherd, He is the Husband of the Bride Zion, and there are many other names which a prophetic imagination may discover. When we pray we want to turn to God, who is beyond our imagination. Jew, Christian and Muslim do not want their prayer to become a human monologue. All three turn to the One God. The Christian, weary of the misinterpretation of Greek monistic thinking, concludes his prayer with the words: 'In the name of the Father, the Son and the Holy Spirit'. This formula makes prayer a dialogue. The words of the human speaker have addressed God and have therefore ceased to be mere human speech and have become prayer.

With the formula 'In the name of the Father, the Son and the Holy Spirit' the fathers of the early Church did not intend to contradict Jewish monotheism, but they meant to oppose Hellenistic heresies. In a time of feverish messianic expectancy a new name of God came into existence. Any name of God is one of the 'thousand names' by which the One Name, the *shem hakodesh*, the holy name of God, can be expressed. The name 'Christ', the name 'Jesus Christ our Lord', the phrase 'In the name of the Father, the Son and the Holy Spirit' can direct the Christian to the One God and can distract him from the One God – as a Christian divine, the profound theologian Kenneth Cragg (1970, p. 24) clearly sees and admits: 'If some in the early Church needed to bring their Christ-devotion more carefully "into God", are there not some in the contemporary Church who need to reach out more readily from their Christology "into God"?' The formula 'In the name of the Father, the Son and the Holy Spirit' is the Christian's Amen. The Muslim's Amen, relating human utterance to God, are the words 'as it is written'. What is the Jew's Amen? It is: 'Amen'.

The early Church pursued the religious aim of preserving monotheism. Eventually a political aim came to the fore which gave the dogma the function of establishing the One Church. By proclaiming that outside the One Church there was no salvation, the Church separated the two monotheistic religions – Judaism and Islam – from Christian monotheism. The theologians were forced by the Christian Emperor to submit to the *raison d'état*. The Pauline dualism – God and Caesar – created the political monotheism, or rather the political monism of the Middle Ages: One God, one emperor, one pope.

All this needed to be said to those Jews, Muslims and also post-medieval men who say that the doctrine of the Trinity is 'incomprehensible'. But our effort to make this dogma comprehensible need not be understood as an apologetical attempt which still regards scholastic metaphysics as a suitable medium for setting out the 'correlation' between God, man and world (Hermann Cohen and Franz Rosenzweig). The scholastic metaphysics which the Church Fathers employed when they formulated the doctrine of the Trinity is out of date. The problems which the doctrine of the Trinity faced are still with us. Hermann Cohen elucidated the correlation between God, man and the world with the help of the triad of human reason: philosophy, ethics and aesthetics. This new method is no longer that of creating with abstract thinking a system of ideas which by a kind of philosophical alchemy give information about God, man and the world. A post-medieval doctrine of the Trinity must express its content not with the help of scholastic metaphysics but with the help of anthropology. This anthropology must view man in his theomorphic reality: man, the image of God. When thinkers leave the Middle Ages, a return to human reality is possible. 'What is man?' is the question that initiates the eternal enquiry. From this beginning we can hope to proceed to the second item of our enquiry: the world. Finally we hope to ascend to the summit and speak about God. This is the way of theological enquiry. But in actual human life it is different. When we start thinking in human life and do so not from playful curiosity but in unreserved commitment, our first thought is God.

THREE CHRISTIAN CIVILIZATIONS

The rise of the *ulema*-rabbi in Israel might be seen as the consequence of an assimilation of the Israeli to his Islamic surroundings. This is not the case. In Israel there is little awareness of Islamic civilization. Israelis meet the Muslim in the encounter of peaceful everyday life and they meet him in the tragic circumstances of battle. Only slowly does an understanding of the world of the Muslim grow. Only a few Jewish intellectuals regard it as their duty to inform themselves about their Muslim cousins.

The rise of the *ulema*-rabbi in Israel can be explained as due to the influence of Anglo-Jewry on Israel. This seems surprising, but it becomes clear as soon as the religious character of Anglo-Jewry is properly analysed. Since its earliest beginnings Anglo-Jewry has lived in the civilization of Petrine Christianity, which is not, like Pauline Christianity, based on *sola fide*, but has a positive attitude to law. Petrine Christianity or, we may say, Petrine civilization dominates the Anglo-Saxon world; Pauline civilization dominates the continent, Germany above all, and Johannine civilization is rooted in the Christianity of the Greek Orthodox Church. In Russia the Christianity of Alyosha, the youngest brother in Dostoevsky's novel *The Brothers Karamazov*, waits for the day of its revival. 'Christianity radiates in three divided directions' (*Star*, p. 402; see also p. 281).

A German Jew who came as a refugee to England was made aware of the difference between Petrine and Pauline civilization when he was asked by his British fellow-Jews: 'Are you a "practising" Jew?' He expected the question: 'Are you a "conscious" Jew?' (*ein bewusster Jude*). Guided by his rabbis to be a 'conscious Jew', the German Jew had acquired a knowledge of the theoretical side of Judaism. To be a practising Jew, on the other hand, meant that a Jew did what the Jewish law demanded of him. The 'conscious Jew' could make his Judaism articulate, the practising Jew obeyed laws. The German Jew assimilated to the Pauline civilization, where *richtige Lehre* (correct doctrine) was pursued with energy. He excelled in writing and reading books about Judaism. The British Jew excelled in mute obedience. He was and still is a 'law-abiding' Jew, alas all too often without scrutinizing the laws and rituals which regulate Jewish life. British Jewry with its small but decisive core of Sephardim did not acquire the capacity to leave the Middle Ages; German Jewry did.

The Petrine Christianity which is the cultural background of Anglo-Jewry is a Christianity with respect for law, and in this it is close to Islam. We can say of the *ulema*-rabbi of Israel that he is influenced by Petrine Christianity. We could also say that he is directly influenced by Islam. The first observation is more apt. There are close connections between Anglo-Jewry and Israel. One thing is clear: with the *ulema*-rabbi in Israel we have stepped outside genuine Judaism and are plagued with all the evils of fundamentalism.

We must point to the danger which surrounds the practising Jew. The true Muslim always 'performs', writes the Christian Islamic scholar Kenneth Cragg (1965, p. 14). What has been called 'practising' by Jews, is called 'performing' by Kenneth Cragg. Whether 'performing' is the right word is to be doubted. It is the word of the scholar who looks on Islam as a Christian. This 'performing' concerns duties towards God: prayer, fasting, almsgiving, in short: *falah*, conduct. In each act of performing, the Muslim submits to the will of God. But moving in our comparison from the devout Muslim to the practising Jew, an ever-present danger becomes visible: what in the case of the Muslim is essentially submission to God, becomes in the practising Jew, who is not also a 'conscious Jew' – mere behaviour. The maxim of the practising Jew is *na'aseh venishma* ('we shall do and hear'). Doing first and listening afterwards can become doing the unimportant, even the wrong thing. The maxim 'we shall do and hear' guides the practising Jew. But if he does not also have knowledge of the meaning of what he does, his Judaism loses the prophetic element and ends up as ritualism.

On the other hand the emphasis on 'knowing', on dogma or doctrine, also has its inherent dangers. We speak today of a 'crisis of faith'. This crisis can be diagnosed as a crisis of Pauline

Christianity. The European record of Pauline Christianity has two dark chapters: first, Luther's cruel pamphlet *Against the Thieving and Murderous Gangs of Peasants* advising the *Fürsten* (princes) to exterminate the followers of Thomas Münzer; and secondly, Karl Barth's and Pius XII's abandonment of the Jews under the Nazis. Luther, translating Romans 3:28, changed 'through faith' into 'through faith alone'. The 'alone' is Luther's copyright. When German pastors approached Karl Barth at Hitler's arrival to power with the question 'What shall we do now?', Barth answered: *'Theologie treiben, als ob nichts geschehen waere'* (Remain engaged in theology, . . . as if nothing had happened). 'As if nothing had happened.' In this Barth is an equal of Pius XII, although a world of difference lies between them. During Pius XII's pontificate nothing was allowed to happen which could have been interpreted as criticism or opposition to Hitler; he ruled the Church like a dictator and watched over the dogma whose teaching goes back to the darkest Middle Ages. The Pope is implicated in the guilt of the genocide of the Jews. It is the guilt of Pauline Christianity that the record of Christianity in the social field is so bad. It is not so much Pauline civilization but Pauline civilization 'alone' which is exposed to this grave indictment. Germany, where Luther's emphasis on *richtige Lehre* was dominant, lay open to invasion by a wicked doctrine which destroyed cities and killed millions. Doctrine 'alone' becomes doctrine without the law of justice and without the spirit of holiness.

We turn now to the third type of Christian civilization, to Johannine Christianity. It has been said that the Gospel of John is more anti-Jewish than the Synoptic Gospels. According to Angelus Silesius, Johannine civilization is the Christian civilization of the future. Rosenzweig accepts this point of view. Goethe, writes Rosenzweig, is the first Christian of the coming Johannine age. But only a few years after Rosenzweig wrote this, Fascism appeared on the horizon of history. Mussolini, Hitler and Stalin meant the end of Johannine civilization, not its beginning. Yet German Jews did become involved in Johannine civilization. How did this happen? How could faithful Jews become influenced by the spiritual gospel, by what is called the third person of the Trinity, by the Holy Spirit?

One would expect the spiritual Christianity of John to have had no influence on Jews. A historic Jesus could be interpreted by Jews as a Messiah, as a rabbi, as a teacher, as an Essene. As long as there was a connection with history, Jews and gospel writers were at least talking from the same premises, although in the end disagreeing. But a spiritual Jesus was inconceivable to Jews. And yet there was the third type of Jew, shaped by Johannine civilization and therefore different from the 'practising Jew', shaped by the Petrine, and from the Jew, whom we called 'conscious Jew', shaped by Pauline civilization, by a Judaism laid down in the writings of the *Wissenschaft des Judentums*. What could be the characteristics of the Jew of Johannine civilization, of a Jew under the impact of spiritual Christianity? Was such a Jew still a Jew? Did he exist? He did. Where Jews of the nineteenth century viewed politics without consideration, even without any realization that politics have something to do with power, they lapsed into a world which lacked connection with reality. Whatever 'spirit' may mean, it means an antithesis to reality. The life and death of the German Jew, Gustav Landauer, represents not only the small group of anarchists to which he belonged. Landauer is typical of a whole noble generation who approached political thinking, debating and organizing from the standpoint of John's maxim: In the beginning was the word. They thought it possible for human society to do without the power of a state and without a police force. Rules should be accepted voluntarily. Laws need not be obeyed because laws should not exist.

A society without enforced laws did come into existence for a short while. Landauer founded a little colony of artists and writers, the archetype of the Israeli kibbutz. Any biography of Martin Buber which fails to show the decisive influence of Gustav Landauer on him is sadly incomplete.

Freemasonry can be called a caricature of Johannine Christianity. But a caricature clarifies the original by distortion. Johannine Christianity is Christianity without dogma and law and in that respect it is similar to Freemasonry. The only dogma of Free-masonry is that there should be no dogma, the only law that there should be no law. In that respect Freemasonry belongs to Johannine civilization. There was a time – as we must assume from Mozart's *Magic Flute* – when Freemasonry gathered serious believers. Landauer was not a Freemason. He followed the teaching of Kropotkin and Tolstoy. He opposed Marxism in the name of a socialism which aimed at a community outside industrial society and outside the state. His *Gegen-Realität* (Anti-Reality) can only be understood in the meaning of the Gospel of John. Spirit is for the Christian *Gegen-Realität*. Landauer was aware of the Christian roots of his anti-Marxist ideology, but in spite of this awareness he did not become baptized. He confessed his spiritual concept of reality passionately, but outside the Church. He was a Jew of Johannine civilization among many others, Jews and Christians, who attacked the political and economic establishment in the name of the spirit – noble men, destined to fail. Landauer's anarchism attacked Marxism in the name of socialism. Of this socialism the German Social Democratic Party had not the slightest understanding. Bebel denounced Landauer at a Party Congress as a police spy. The Prussian police, on the other hand, hounded Landauer as an anarchist, and Landauer, who had undergone spells of imprisonment in Germany, fled to England in 1901 and spent two quiet years in Bromley, translating and writing.

In one respect Landauer differed from his fellow-anarchists. He rejected the concept of free love. The covenant of marriage is to Landauer both a spiritual and a material relationship and thereby the archetype of the unenforced and therefore human bond between man and man in all spheres. 'My home, my castle, my wife, my children – my world.' What made this island a reality? Landauer answers: it is the spirit. The spirit is both non-reality and the force which creates reality.

Landauer was murdered in the Munich counter-revolution of 1918. The murderers were German fascists. The killers vindicated the belief that politics must use force. 'In the beginning was the word . . . the darkness comprehended it not.' The word, the *Logos* of Philo, the spirit which the Gospel of John preached, shaped Jews, the Jews of the Johannine civilization. The dictatorships made it their paramount programme to purge their state of any man of Johannine bent, be he Jew or non-Jew. Landauer's circle was but a small one. But the history of German Jewry, indeed the German history of the 'poets and thinkers', gave birth to a whole generation of Jews who, side by side with the 'conscious Jew', and the 'practising Jew', are a type of their own. In the kibbutzim of Israel they live on. They are not to be confused with conscientious objectors or pacifists. They have proved this again recently as soldiers in the Six Day War. But when, in the evening after a day's hard work, they discuss politics, they are still Jews of the type of Gustav Landauer.

About Landauer's last hour we have the report of an eyewitness and of various informed contemporaries. There was a benign smile on his face. He had always known that his entry into the political struggle could only lead to his death. Jews die with the 'Hear, O Israel' on their lips. What did the benign smile on his face say? His last words were: '*O Menschen, O Menschen!*' (O mankind, O mankind!). Before the soldiers started clubbing and shooting, they made him take off his coat. Their spoil must not be stained by the blood of their victim. Did the benign smile have its origin in the parallel with the Gospel story? The Jew serving the gentiles in Johannine civilization suffers the Christian predicament. For Paul the highest ideal is belief with love at its side; for Peter it is love and law; for John it is the spirit. In the family these three – love, law, spirit – are experienced together. Landauer dies for one of the three: for the spirit. The Jew confesses the unity of God. The three are one. In Christian civilization man encounters a trinity. When the Jew leaves his father's house and enters history, he becomes involved in, even committed to, Pauline, Petrine and Johannine civilization.

SHYLOCK, THE TRAGIC CHAMPION OF THE LAW

The Merchant of Venice belongs to Shakespeare's 'problem comedies'. The problem in this play is the clash between justice and mercy, between law and love. In its attitude to love and mercy Judaism does not contradict Christianity. Islam does. Shakespeare is the playwright who stands in the age of the Renaissance. But he is also highly praised for his thorough understanding of the Middle Ages. As I have pointed out in preceding chapters, in the Middle Ages Christians identified the Jew with the Muslim. Shylock's belief in the ultimate validity of a written law is characteristic of the Muslim. The Jewish attitude to law is different. But Shakespeare's Shylock is introduced as a Jew who has an absolute belief in the concept of law. 'I crave the law', 'I stand here for law', says Shylock. Driven into a corner by Portia, Shylock asks: 'Is that the law?' He asks this question in humble submission: the law must be obeyed; the law is the letter of the law; there is no way out. This is Islamic belief. Judaism, on the other hand, has since the Pharisaic interpretation of the concept of law a different approach to legal arguments. One has only to turn to the traditional texts and one will find a way out of every dilemma; the wisdom of the law, of the Torah that is, is inexhaustible. 'Turn it [the Torah] again and again, because everything is in it' (*Abot*, v, 25).

In Jonathan Miller's production (The National Theatre, London, 1970), with Laurence Olivier as Shylock, Jessica stands in the last scene on the darkened stage, silent and motionless, holding a sheet of paper – the law. As she looks at it she faces the merciless legal inevitability. The law, however hurtful to man, cannot be changed. The Muslim accepts this situation in submission. The Jewish understanding of the law makes no such inhuman demand. Jewish casuistry becomes an instrument of mercy; interpretation becomes liberation from the rigours of a written law. In Shakespeare's portrayal of Shylock, the difference between Jew and Muslim does not always come to light. Under the conditions of the Middle Ages this difference often disappeared, and Jew and Muslim stood undifferentiated in the Christian world. Shakespeare is therefore not wrong in ascribing Muslim features to the Jew Shylock.

The Marx Brothers, philosophical clowns of great human insight, reveal the Jewish attitude to the law. In one of their films one brother holds a huge piece of paper with all the clauses of a contract in his hands. As they negotiate, they tear strip after strip of paper off the long roll of the document until they reduce it to nothing. This clowning is profound, and it is symbolic that it is brought on to the screen by Jews. Jews feel that written laws can and must be interpreted for use in daily life until they cease to be harmful. Modern Orthodox Jews do not have such a liberal approach; in petrified tradition they uphold the medieval situation in which Jews were influenced by Islamic civilization. The Jewish law, the Talmudic rabbis said, is a 'law of mercy'. The clownery of the Marx Brothers made these rabbis visible on the screen; Shakespeare makes the Islamic obedience to the law visible on the stage.

The law as the antithesis to love brought Islam on the stage of world history as the opponent of Christianity. The Jew, representing the faith which is the seed bringing forth Christianity and Islam, can sometimes appear near to Islam, sometimes near to Christianity. He is not involved in the Christian opposition to Islam, or in the Islamic opposition to Christianity. Culturally such involvements exist. There were parts of Jewish history in which Islam, other parts in which Christianity, shaped the cultural frame of Jewish life. Islam stands in the background of Maimonides' life and work, Christianity in the background of Franz Rosenzweig's.

Shylock's insistence on the law – 'my bond, my bond' – is manly morality. He must not be played as a monster. He has greatness, the greatness of moral conviction. 'What judgment shall I dread doing no wrong?' 'I stand for judgment, – answer, shall I have it?' No respectable puritan could address judge and jury with a more impressive display of moral integrity! Shylock does not beg for mercy. He can rely on the law. He stands for the law like any Muslim. A written law has been brought from heaven and given by God to the Muslim believers. The law is the holy law.

The popular concept of the Jew, which is represented to the full in Marlowe's play *The Jew of Malta* was overcome by Shakespeare. Marlowe's Jew was comical, cruel, satanic. Shakespeare had to reckon with the fact that an Elizabethan audience, though they hardly met real Jews, would see Shylock in this way. But Shakespeare, being Shakespeare, changes the monster of the fairy tale into a human being before our very eyes. The laughter freezes on the faces of the watching audience, and behold! – they become passionate witnesses. They see a suffering man, a Jew in the hands of cruel Christians. Portia pleads that if law is adduced as an argument against mercy, it is cruel. Her plea for mercy has the glowing fervour and the sweet persuasiveness of I Corinthians 13:1: 'I may speak in tongues of men or of angels, but if I am without love, I am a sounding gong or a clanging cymbal.' Here Paul attempts to translate the word *rachmanut* (mercy) for a Greek-speaking audience. He succeeds, as far as success is possible here. So does Shakespeare in Portia's speech: 'The quality of mercy . . .' But their success lies in the words which Paul and Shakespeare find to enhance the importance of a Christian doctrine. *Rachmanut* is not a doctrine, it is more a bodily response than a mere cerebral expression. One can mentally approve of mercy and at the same time fail to live up to the human response which mercy demands. Portia proves this. After reciting her wonderful hymn on mercy she is most cruel towards Shylock. To show mercy is the demand of the Christian dogma. The Muslim obeys laws, not dogmas. Mercy is also an Islamic law. God, Allah, is *al-Rahim*, the compassionate one.

It is debatable whether mankind benefits more from the dogma of mercy or from the law of mercy. Where the treatment of Jews is concerned, Islam was merciful to those outside its denominational walls. To the Muslim, Jews were infidels. So were Christians. But Jews and Christians were both respected as 'people of the Book' and given a place in humanity by Islam. Christianity with its *nulla salus extra ecclesiam* did not grant a Muslim or a Jew a place in humanity up to Vatican II. They were seen as the Elizabethan mob saw Shylock, as wicked people, as monsters.

Rachmanut, the Hebrew word for mercy, denotes neither a dogma nor a law. It means a human reaction of both a bodily and a spiritual nature. True man reacts with *rachmanut*. The more man is man, the more he is capable of and open to the warm feeling and quick response of *rachmanut*. Man created in the image of God and preserving this image in himself is always fraught with waves of *rachmanut*, that mercy which is an attribute of both God and man. *Rachmanut* is neither a dogma nor a law, but is that truly human experience of man, which the dogma of mercy and the law of mercy try to make articulate.

Shylock the Jew is the warm-hearted Jew, who, we feel, knows both the call of *rachmanut* and the majesty which the law wields. He appears as the father of a daughter. True, Marlowe in his *Jew of Malta* also tells a story of father and daughter. But the story is not credible. Fairy-tale villains may make the audience's flesh creep in terror. But at no moment is the fairy-tale taken as reality. Shakespeare makes us look into reality. A Muslim wants sons. Daughters are not greeted at birth with particular joy. But Shylock loves Jessica. He remembers Leah, his deceased wife. He remembers the years of his courtship. He worries about Jessica's future, distrusting Christian husbands. When Bassanio admits that he would be able to sacrifice his love for Portia for the sake of another love, that for Antonio, Shylock is disgusted. Marriage, initiated and preserved by love, is always safeguarded by law. Shylock stands for law. He mistrusts a 'love affair' as basis for marriage. Poor Jessica, the Jewish girl among Christians!

> These be the Christian husbands! I have a daughter –
> Would any of the stock of Barabbas
> had been her husband, rather than a Christian.
> (Act IV, Sc. 1)

Love exalts the children of man. 'Love is strong as death' (S. of S. 8:6). Law gives security. Law provides stability both in marriage and in all the various transactions of a great city such as Venice. Jew and Muslim respect the majesty of the law. Love is not bound by law. Love is lawless love. Youth needs the protection of the law against love. Poor Jessica – a Jewish girl alone, un-protected in the world of Christians.

The Muslim rejects the spiritual concept of love. As for the Jew, he knows that even the non-spiritual can be holy; he acknowledges love not as being spiritual but as being holy. The words 'My sister, my bride' in the Song of Songs 4:9 have been understood by Jews both as a dialogue between God and Israel and as a dialogue between man and woman in love. These words are not spoken in the realm of Christian love which does not, indeed must not be fulfilled in the cohabitation of the two sexes. Christian love is not consummated love. This cruel spirituality hurts the female partner more than the male. Shylock sees Jessica in the cruel world of Christian love. He weeps over Jessica, who has not listened to the warning in the Song of Songs against permissiveness: 'I adjure you, O daughters of Jerusalem . . . that ye awake not nor stir up love until it please . . .' (2:7). Now Jessica is with a Christian man who, not uniting love and law, will not be able to soothe his girl with the words 'My sister, my bride!' Love and law, which cannot be united doctrinally, can be united where both heart and mind are alive and make up human behaviour.

Shylock is a Jewish father, mourning the loss of a daughter. In the noble Belgravia of Venice, in Belmont, Shylock's rejection of lawless love is repeated in another key, in the language of poetry and music:

> Tell me where is Fancy bred
> Or in the heart, or in the head?
> How begot, how nourished?
> (Act III, Sc. 2)

In Shakespearian English, fancy means love. In Belgravia Venice, in Belmont, the answer to the question concerning love is the same as the answer which would be given by the law-abiding puritans of the merchant city of Venice themselves. We can safely put the words of Proverbs 31:30 into their tight-lipped mouths: 'Charm is a delusion and beauty fleeting: it is the God-fearing woman who is honoured.' We are even allowed the suspicion that Portia directs Bassanio with the song 'Tell me where is Fancy bred . . .' to by-pass gold and silver in the lottery of the caskets and to choose lead. The little song distinguishes between illusion and reality in the Christian Manichean distrust of reality and of love of the flesh. In this Shylock and Portia, although different as Jew and Christian, come to the same view concerning love. 'Head and heart', law and ecstasy, fight a battle where love takes hold of man. Love

> . . . is engend'red in the eyes,
> With gazing fed . . .
> (Act III, Sc. 2)

The Christian is no longer in the Hebrew tradition, but is a captive of Greece where the eye provides the momentary revelation. Love sees heaven open, is faith, nourished by faith, and is certainly not based on law. But the Hebrew view is expressed in the line which is a dirge about the death of love.

> . . . Fancy dies
> In the cradle where it lies: . . .
> Let us all ring Fancy's knell . . .
> (Act III, Sc. 2)

Human life without the direction of law ends in destruction. Human life without love is unthinkable. As father and husband Shylock testifies to the holiness of love. The bridegroom in the Song of Songs testifies to the holiness of love when he, in the midst of his passion, says 'My sister, my bride!'

The love-law issue dominates merry Belgravia-Belmont itself. In the humorous ring scene an assumed infidelity is taken lightly. Permissive tolerance, not the strict rule of the law, seems to be the code of Belmont's youth. The inscription on one of the two rings reads 'Love me but leave me not.' In the dialogue between the two principal lovers of the play, Portia and Bassanio, the often-repeated word 'ring', 'ring', 'ring' does not sound like a severe reproach, but like a warning uttered in friendly understanding. Nothing has happened, and nothing, it is understood, will happen. It is all a joke. What is missing in Belgravia-Belmont is the seriousness which the word 'law' denotes to Jew and Muslim. Surely, the repetition of the word 'ring' is a reminder of what the law stands for. But Belgravia-Belmont seems smilingly to forgive, where Jew and Muslim adopt a puritanical outlook in respect of marriage. A Muslim girl says to a male who is eyeing her: 'Fear God, I am a virgin.' Would the merry youth of Belgravia-Belmont not giggle and snigger at the puritanical Muslim girl? The Old Testament values virginity; ascetic discipline in the pre-marital state is recommended to the youth of both sexes. There are instances in which Jewish and Muslim law provide important protection to daughters and wives. The spiritual sublimity in the picture of the Madonna can impart a status of inferiority to ordinary women who are more connected with earthly nature than men. To the medieval Christian, women were mere chattels, they had no place in the Christian society governed by celibate priests. What will happen to Jessica in a Christian world? Shylock is sorely aggrieved.

Antonio is both a Jew-hater and a Christian, cherishing spiritual love. A Freudian might see suppressed homosexuality in Antonio's love of Bassanio. Because of this view the Freudian will be called 'Jew' with the anti-Semitic contempt added to the word 'Jew'. Antonio need not be seen as a homosexual. His love is spiritual love, love not consummated in the sexual act. The love between Tristan and Isolde is not, indeed, must not become love consummated in marriage. 'Wagner: background music for a pogrom', writes Saul Bellow (*Mr Sammler's Planet*). Saul Bellow's sharp criticism need not be understood as a denigration of Wagner's great art. He is a truly Christian artist, as Kierkegaard is a truly Christian theologian. Both interpret love as Christian Manicheans. Jew and Muslim may not understand such an attitude. Their lack of understanding will be irksome to Christians of the brand of Kierkegaard. Christians will even hate those who refuse to acknowledge, let alone approve of, the spiritual quality of love. The Christian, distinguishing between spiritual and secular, does not regard Jew and Muslim, who distinguish between holy and profane, merely as belonging to a different school of thought. The Christian, uplifted to his spiritual realm, reacts with hatred to those who differ from him and deny what he regards as the truth, as the basis of his existence. Here the

Christian cannot simply agree to differ. Here anti-Semitism is built into Christian faith. True, the Christian who upholds his belief and turns to a spiritual existence is more a Manichean Christian than a Christian as the dogma of the Church understands him. The dogma of the Church, accepting the Old Testament, was forced to turn a somersault and to come to terms with the anti-Semitic hatred built into Christianity. Thus there is hope for a Jewish-Christian understanding. But those who work for this understanding have courageously to face the Jew-hatred of the Christian. Antonio also teaches us that 'sadness', as Shakespeare calls it, is built into the Christian way of life. He confesses

> I hold the world . . .
> A stage, where every man must play a part,
> And mine a sad one.
>
> (Act I, Sc. 1)

Spiritual uplift says farewell to life, as ordinary humans live it. Christian saints and ordinary Christian believers derive happiness from their spiritual way of life. But it is a sad happiness. It is a happiness, plucked from a sad withdrawal from the world. The happiness of the Psalmist, on the other hand, is happiness in the midst of unchanged reality: in marriage, in fatherhood, in motherhood, in the family, in short, in an ordinary way of life. Christians of the type of Kierkegaard, Schopenhauer and Wagner regarded the patriarchs in the Book of Genesis, who led this way of life, as bourgeois.

How annoying that these 'Jewish materialists' refused to see reality as illusion. Schopenhauer expressed his Christian Jew-hatred when he spoke of 'cursed Jewish optimism'. Sociology and psychology cannot succeed in explaining anti-Semitism.

Theology has to be consulted in order to explain Christian Jew-hatred. Jewish and Islamic unbelief in the face of the miracle of the transfiguration through love – Wagner's *Liebestod* and the Cross, symbolizing not death, but resurrection – remains the scandal which every Jew represents by his very existence. No true Christian can feel at ease facing what is *skandalon*, the scandal, in Christian eyes. Here the Jew has nothing with which to appease the Christian anti-Semite. But he can say to him: Mind your stumbling-block.

In Shakespeare's play the medieval form of *disputatio* is discarded. Instead, Jew and Christian face each other: the one not really representing only the teachings of his Church, the other not really representing only the Torah, the teachings of the Synagogue. Jew and Christian are two types of man. The clash occurs not merely between representatives of two different doctrinal systems. The Christian is a man whose humanity is Christian, just as the Jew is a man whose humanity is Jewish. This means Jew and Christian meet in Shakespeare's play on the same level. In all walks of life, in business, in war, in his private life, in love and in marriage, the Christian acts as a Christian, the Jew as a Jew.

Can a leopard change his spots? Can a Christian leave the Jew alone, who refuses to give up his being different from the Christian? Is this refusal of the Jew to become a Christian merely the rejection of Christian doctrine? What does Shylock know about the details of Jewish law? He is not a rabbi. A rabbi would teach Shylock that the 'righteous of the gentiles' are justified in the eyes of God. A rabbi would demand from Shylock to stop hating and to stop pursuing revenge. Shylock is a Jew hated by Christians, and he responds to the hatred of his persecutors with the hatred of the persecuted. 'I hate him for he is a Christian' (Act I, Sc. 3), says Shylock of Antonio. No redeeming distinction is made between gentile and Christian. The cruel gentile and the Christian are seen inseparably as one character, and the persecuted Jew ends up as a hater. The Christian made him that. But Shylock hates the gentiles, not, as he says, the Christians. The Christian Jew-hatred, on the other hand, is directed against the Jew, against the Jew with his Jewish faith. Peace between Jew and Christian can only be achieved by the Christian on one condition: the Jew must be forced to become a Christian. The unbaptized Jew is an offence to the Christian; the Jew denies what the Christian believes. Christian Jew-hatred cannot be resolved. Shylock leaves it at that. His noble speech 'Hath not a Jew eyes? . . .' is humanism. It is spoken to the gallery, to people who are shaped more by the Renaissance than by the Christian Church. But with his 'I will not . . . pray with you' Shylock makes it clear that he is not a humanist. He is a Jew. He prays to God. The humanist does not and is not able to do so.

I was reminded of Shakespeare's penetrating new insight in the Jewish-Christian relationship, when I spoke on a platform for Jewish-Christian fellowship. Whenever I used the expression 'the Christians' I saw a shadow of annoyance come over the face of my Christian chairman. Had I said something disagreeable? So it seemed. My Christian friend, a staunch Methodist, would not -have minded hearing critical references to the historical Church. He himself indulged in them. But he had nothing to do with these sins of the Church. He felt himself a Christian, an exponent of an unassailable doctrine. But then he heard my 'the Christians'. This dragged him from his doctrinal ivory tower on to the stage where Christians are exposed to the world like the Jews and are exposed in their hatred and love and recognized in the open marketplace in their human behaviour without the fig leaf of doctrinal justification. Hatred is not theoretical or doctrinal disagreement. Hatred is the most murderous weapon of the persecutor. The number of martyrs in our time grew to millions. Hatred had risen from the dark recesses of Christian souls.

I have no desire to indulge in apologetics, which undertake to whitewash what is black. The history of religion has its numerous black chapters. But does Shylock speak as a Jew, when he says: 'I hate him for he is a Christian'? It is the stage-Jew, the Jew as the mob imagines him, not the Jew whose humanity Shakespeare has discovered with the eyes of a genius, and with his heart, which sees the image of God in every human creature. The Christian Jew-hatred, on the other hand, is a fact proved by two thousand years of Christianity. Hatred of the Christians cannot be established as a historical characteristic of the Jewish people. A novel, *Dre Weg ohne Ende* ('The Way without End'), by the German Jew, Gerson Stern (1934), impressively proves the absence of hatred of Christians in Jews. In this novel a Christian lad says to a Jew who has just suffered an anti-Semitic abuse from a Christian, 'you must really hate us.' The Jewish answer is: 'If we were to hate, we could not live.'

Shakespeare's *Merchant of Venice* speaks of Jews and Christians. In fact, the play shows persecutors and persecuted. It shows the Christian as persecutor. Yet Christian doctrine must not be denounced as a superstructure simply overlaying material interests. The doctrine of Christian love becomes the mighty motive for superhuman action. Following the doctrine of Christian love the Christian nurse overcomes the heavy burden she carries day and night, the Christian missionary dares to go forward into the jungle and into barbarian surroundings, and the Christian soldier sacrifices his life in order to defend the freedom and wellbeing of his kith and kin.

Shylock is a Jew! Antonio is a Christian! Bassanio, Portia and the others are not merely citizens of Venice. They are Christians. Shylock has his Jewish gabardine, the Italian noble citizens have their Jew-hatred. Jew-hatred is 'the mark of *their* tribe'. In Jonathan Miller's production, the Jewish gabardine was replaced by the respectable coat of the Victorian banker. But the Jew-hatred undergoes no change. It has been the same throughout all the centuries of Christianity.

The Christian is the noble member of the establishment. The Christian in the lowest station of life feels superior to the Jew, who is and remains a foreigner. Shakespeare marked Shylock as a foreigner through the name he invented for him. These are the names of the gentlemen of Belmont: Antonio, Bassanio, Lorenzo, Gobbo, all of them ending with the letter O; the names of the women have an A as their last letter: Portia, Nerissa and Jessica – already assimilated through her name to the noble crowd which will later receive her as an equal. The name 'Shylock' does not fit into the society of Belmont. It is an embarrassment; Shakespeare chose well. When in the court scene the duke commands 'Antonio and old Shylock, both stand forth', Portia knows very well who is Antonio and who Shylock. But in icecold approach she asks: 'Is your name Shylock?', and Shylock has to reply, as if to admit a wrong: 'My name is Shylock.' He is singled out through his very name. What is his crime? He is a foreigner.

'God loves the foreigner.' This is what Jewish Holy Scripture tells us (Deut. 10:18). The laws of Venice protect the foreigner. But in the whole play of Shakespeare not a single word of love is said, not a single act of love is shown to Shylock by anybody. They only hate him, mock him, despise him. Shylock responds in the same way. His rebellion against his tormentors is just as articulate as his conviction that he is seen, protected, and indeed revenged by God. Summing up the various passages about the Servant of God in the Book of Isaiah, we feel prompted to say: The Servant may very well have had experiences not so different from those of Shylock. The Servant of God faces hatred, scorn and contempt. Shylock carries his burden with normal human reactions. When the play ends, Shylock is still alive. We are allowed to ponder about his fate after the fifth act. Shakespeare and the Bible! The great Shakespeare stops with the fifth act. The Bible has narratives which lead the reader beyond the fifth act. Where Shakespeare has no hope to offer, the Bible offers hope. Shylock's, the Jew's, survival offers hope to all men. Shakespeare's Shylock is nothing but a man. A Jew is nothing but a man, loving his kin, suffering pain and reacting to love and hatred as any man does. A man of this kind, an ordinary man, Everyman can – after the fifth act – achieve the holy station, in which the Book of Isaiah introduces the Servant of God to us. The Jewish survivor of a pogrom can and will often be a broken man, a Shylock in the fifth act. But, as he has not been killed but still lives, he can leave the fifth act behind and proceed to the holiness which the Christian worships in the symbol of the Cross and which in Jewish everyday life is holiness become reality.

The actor Paul Rogers played Shylock in a mask whose features reminded me and others of the conventional Christ-face. Shylock, a victim delivered into the hands of cruel torturers! The modern audience of Shakespeare has become mature. Shylock with his red wig, Shylock as an objectionable character, has disappeared from the stage. Laurence Olivier plays a Shylock who is impressive in his conformity with pious Jewish ritual. He wears a skull-cap, he has a prayer shawl at hand and, in the sad moment when the loss of Jessica has to be accepted as final, the audience hears the sombre tune of the *Kaddish* prayer. Jonathan Miller's production brings Shylock on the stage as a pious Jew. He is pious like Job, thundering words to heaven about his misfortune, a Lear deserted, a dethroned king. He is always greater than the businessmen of Venice and the idle crowd drawn to Belmont.

The 'usurer' Shylock angered a Victorian Jewish audience and still annoys American Jews. Today we understand the 'financier' Shylock. The acquisitive man can be reproached with religious arguments, but is today also recognized as a guardian of the competitive, that is, the free society. The communist world may have checked the acquisitiveness of man, but at too costly a price: communist society is without freedom. 'Usury' is taken by a modern audience of Shakespeare as the old-fashioned term for interest on capital. What is wrong with Shylock's usury? The Bank of England announces the interest rate at intervals and makes it known how much 'usury' is granted to those who give loans. This is the capitalist era which was just being ushered in in Shylock's days in place of the feudal economy. Money replaced land as the measure of value. The medieval Christian was Manichean: the world was evil, money and sex were the very elements of an evil world. But the new age of bourgeois values put an end to the aristocratic style of life. The gaiety, ease and colourful scenery of Belmont rests on – money. Money breeds money. This still shocked Elizabethan society, which itself only slowly and painfully awoke to the rise of capitalism. Shylock represents the new age. A modern audience of *The Merchant of Venice* is no longer inclined to despise a representative of the acquisitive society. That is what Shylock is. R. H. Tawney (1925) is the pioneer for a fair understanding of Shylock. 'Which is the Merchant here? and which the Jew?' (Act 4, Sc. 1) asks Portia, disguised as a young doctor of law. The distinction between the royal merchant Antonio and the Jew, the moneylender, is difficult to make. Antonio in his distaste for usury lends money without interest. But where does his money come from that permits such generosity, such 'Christian courtesy'? From his argosies, his ships, in short, from his trade. Antonio, the merchant, is also dedicated to making money, to profit. And profit when analysed, is often 'usury' in a more respectable form. Antonio, despising Shylock, is acting in self-hatred. 'Wilt thou whip thine own fault in other men?' cries Timon of Athens, in another play of Shakespeare (see Goddard, 1969, p. 148). But there remains the outcry: 'My daughter! O my ducats! O my daughter!' (Act II, Sc. 8). Do these words not make Shylock a monster? It is often forgotten that we do not hear Shylock say these words. They are brought to our knowledge in a report by Solanio who tells us that Shylock, driven in his pain to the frenzy of madness, runs about, muttering and crying 'Justice, the law, my ducats, and my daughter!' (ibid.). He addresses nobody, he is oblivious of 'All the boys of Venice', who follow him and witness in the breakdown of the old man a scene which attracts their cruel curiosity. A breakdown, a madness which robs the old man of his senses, makes him curse: 'I would my daughter were dead at my foot, and the jewels in her ear: would she were hears'd at my foot, and the ducats in her coffin' (Act III, Sc. 1). It has to be remembered that Shylock does not speak here as a rational being. True, these words come out of his mouth. But a raging passion drives him to utter this curse. The cursing old man reveals himself as a man of deep emotion. He loves his daughter. He is the father betrayed by his child, whom he never stops loving. In the moment of unbearable grief he curses his beloved child. In his powerless state man has only one way out. Blessing and cursing, like love and hate, lie near to each other in man's heart. The cursing Shylock of the third act is Shylock in the moment of greatest tragic pain. But in spite of the curse, Shylock will not cease to be the loving father. When in Jonathan Miller's production Shylock leaves the stage after the court scene (Act IV, Sc. 1), he cries out in pain like an animal, mourning the loss of his daughter. He is no longer seen but his cry of anguish is heard. This inarticulate cry repeats Jeremiah's lament: 'Rachel weeping for her children. She refuses to be comforted, they are no more' (31:15).

The actor Schildkraut, as a Jew committed to vindicating the humanity of Shylock, played a father who remained unforgettable to those who saw him on the stage. Although the old man babbles and mutters, unceasingly lamenting the stolen treasures, only his daughter, who has left him, is in his mind. Schildkraut's way of acting this role is justified. But Shakespeare requires us to live up to his genius. To Shylock, the persecuted, offended, despised man, to this down-trodden human being, to this man in the depth of distress, everything is the same: money – jewels – the memory of his youth and of Leah, his deceased wife, and his daughter – all this is his life. He knows of no life beyond his home and his family, beyond his house, his 'sober house' and beyond the money which he had earned, for the sake of his home and his family. Therefore after the flight of his daughter he does not know what he should lament first. Solanio, who reports this situation to us, characterizes Shylock's behaviour as 'a passion so confused' and tells us that the words uttered by Shylock were 'so strange, outrageous . . . !'

> My daughter! O my ducats! O my daughter!
> Fled with a Christian! O my Christian ducats!
> Justice, the law, my ducats, and my daughter!
> (Act II, Sc. 8)

Such is Solanio's report. The world sees Shylock as Solanio describes him.

Jago, Edmund, Richard III, the King in Hamlet argue in a monologue about themselves in retrospect. As opposed to these heroes of Shakespeare, Shylock is not heard in a monologue. We see him only as one who reacts to the world. The world forced him into the money business, the world robbed him of money and home, the world despised him, when he progressed from feudal into bourgeois economy. The world mocked him in his suffering. The world, the hostile world, has made Shylock. But behind the Shylock whom the sins of the world have made into what he is, behind the Shylock whom the world abhors, is Shylock the man. If this man is a monster, he is a monster in the sense in which the Servant of God is one:

> he had no beauty, no majesty to draw our eyes, no grace to make us delight in him; his form, disfigured, lost all the likeness of man, his beauty changed beyond human semblance. He was despised, he shrank from the sight of men, tormented and humbled by suffering;

we despised him, we held him of no account, a thing from which men turn away their eyes. Yet . . . the Lord laid upon him the guilt of us all (Isa. 53 : 2, 3, 6).

Gustav Landauer (1920) writes in his book on Shakespeare that he has seen productions of *The Merchant of Venice* in which the actors added to the play their own, genuine, interpretation in the following way: In several productions Shylock returns to his empty house, with a lamp in his hand. We only see the light, the house is in full darkness. The light moves from the ground floor to the top, from one room to the next: the old man searches in vain for his daughter. But in his mad search, in the light flickering in the darkness, we get Shakespeare's message: behold, a Jew, robbed by the Christians of his beloved child !

Shylock is forced to become a Christian. Baptism or death – that was the Christian alternative for Jews throughout the Middle Ages. Jessica, too, becomes a Christian. But her conversion is according to the rules of a new age in which Christian culture, not the Christian Church, makes Christians different from Jews. Lorenzo teaches Jessica that art assists man in becoming a Christian. When Jessica contradicts her Christian tutor Lorenzo with the words 'I am never merry, when I hear sweet music', she is still the Jewish girl, daughter of her puritanical father. He has warned her before:

> Let not the sound of shallow fopp'ry enter
> My sober house . . .
>
> (Act II, Sc. 5)

But Lorenzo is constant in his lesson about Christianity. 'Sit Jessica', he says, and begins with a hymn on music, which converts the wild gentiles into gentle men.

> Since naught so stockish, hard, and full of rage,
> But music for the time doth change his nature.
> The man that hath no music in himself,
> Nor is not mov'd with concord of sweet sounds,
> Is fit for treasons, stratagems, and spoils;
> The motions of his spirit are dull as night,
> And his affections dark as Erebus:
> Let no such man be trusted.
>
> (Act V, Sc. 1)

He means: Do not trust the Jews. The whole cosmos – according to Lorenzo – proves the truth of the Christian faith.

> Sit Jessica. Look how the floor of heaven
> Is thick inlaid with patens of bright gold:
> There's not the smallest orb which thou behold'st
> But in his motion like an angel sings,
> Still quiring to the young-eyed cherubins;
> Such harmony is in immortal souls;
> But whilst this muddy vesture of decay
> Doth grossly close it in, we cannot hear it.
>
> (Act V, Sc. 1)

'Patens' are the small flat dishes used in Holy Communion. In using this word, Lorenzo finds the image of God in culture. Jessica, made fit for Belmont, enters not merely a civilization new to her, she enters Christianity. She forgets the message of the 'Hear, O Israel', which says that no civilization, no culture is identical with the holiness and absoluteness of God: God is One. Jessica becomes a Christian. A new form of baptism is presented to us by Shakespeare.

Yet Belmont is not what the medieval Christian Church was. It is a place of Christian civilization. Therefore Jessica's future remains in the balance. She may or may not become converted to the Christian faith. Shakespeare is not definite about it and leaves the situation open to either possibility. The Christian faith of Lorenzo – man in his 'muddy vesture of decay' – is Manichaean Christianity and therefore irreconcilable with everything Jessica has received from her Jewish past.

On her return Portia greets the light coming from the little candle in her hall with the words:

> How far that little candle throws his beams!
> So shines a good deed in a naughty world.
>
> (Act V, Sc. 1)

With this sentiment she proves to be near to the world of the puritanical Jews. Belmont is, after all, not entirely Belgravia or Mayfair, not entirely Bloomsbury or Hampstead. Belmont too is a place on which the law has its hold. We can hope for Jessica. Jessica is of course pressed by Lorenzo to follow him into his faith. 'Come, Jessica!' But it remains open whether she follows him in true conversion, or whether she does it at all. Jessica, not really converted, Shylock, though robbed of his wealth, still alive – the Jew in the audience of Shakespeare's *Merchant of Venice* can leave after the fifth act and can still hope.

Heine saw it like this:

> Shakespeare would have written a satire against Christianity, if he had made it consist of characters who are enemies of Shylock, but who are hardly worthy to unlace his shoes. Antonio a weak creature without energy . . . Bassanio a fortune hunter . . . Lorenzo accomplice of a most infamous theft . . . the other noble Venetians do not seem to have any special antipathy to money, and when their poor friend is in difficulties, they have nothing for him but words . . . (see Wilders, 1969, pp. 19, 29).

When Heine saw the play performed in Drury Lane, he heard at the end of the fourth act a lady passionately crying out many times: 'The poor man is wronged!' Heine tells us: 'I have never been able to forget them, those great black eyes which wept for Shylock.'

Blessed are the eyes which weep for Shylock.

CHAPTER III

The Home-coming of the Humanist

HUMANISM AS MONOTHEISTIC HERESY

> O Zarathustra, you are more
> pious than you think. (Nietzsche)

It is advisable to begin an assessment of humanism with the acknowledgment that in no case must humanism be rejected outright by those who belong to one of the three monotheistic religions. There is often good reason to speak of Jewish, Christian and Islamic humanism and to understand the attributes Jewish, Christian, Islamic as truly justifiable. It may be that in these three cases the humanist can be called a heretic, but only in the positive sense of I Corinthians 11:19 where we read of a defence of heresies: 'Heresies there must be', says Paul. Since any dogmatic attempt to bring the relationship between God and man into a closed theoretical system must at one point or another become too narrow and must necessarily fail, heresies can help to prevent stagnation. Heresies object to the intellectual system and to the social institution from which they originate but also affirm the truth and adequacy of the preceding established order which they seem to leave behind. Only in this sense can humanism be called a monotheistic heresy. Humanism could not arise in a civilization shaped by Buddhism; only in one shaped by monotheism.

The great merit of the humanist heresy is its revolution against medieval metaphysics, against a philosophy and theology, supposed to possess a volume of subtle thoughts, which saw God as a possible object of knowledge, and regarded revelation as necessary only for simple people. Humanism dethroned scholasticism and thereby brought the Middle Ages to an end. Humanism will not be able to build up the new era. In this new era man stands in the centre. Theology has become anthropology. The question which man cannot help asking: 'What about God?' is bound up with the other question: 'What is man?' The answer reads: 'And God created man in His own image, in the image of God created He him, male and female created He them' (Gen. 1:27). Man has two natures: he is created, is a creature made by God, and he is also something else; he is, as man, the image of God. Man has a human and at the same time a divine nature. Psalm 8 registers them both. The Psalmist asks: 'What is man, that Thou art mindful of him?' The question rises out of deep concern but not out of despair. The final word is triumphant: 'Thou hast made him but little lower than the angels.'

I have just used the phrase 'two natures'. I could have looked for a different, perhaps better, term. But I have chosen this expression to introduce a historical parallel to the controversy about humanism. There is humanism as it grows harmoniously from monotheism. There is also the fierce controversy which rages between the different types of humanism: liberal humanism, atheistic and agnostic humanism, Marxist humanism, Marxist-Leninist humanism. They fight each other as did the various sects led by the Fathers of the Church. The main issue with them was also about an understanding of two natures. Is Christ wholly divine or wholly human or both?

'It was an ignoble fight.' In this and in the following quotations I refer to Christian authors, who are specialists in the history of the Christian dogma. 'Pettiness', 'spite', 'hatred' of church officials and pious people mark the doctrinal struggles of the Church Fathers. The defenders and opponents of the doctrine of the 'two natures' were swayed in their hostility against each other* just as liberals and communists are today. The mob in the streets

---

* *Religion in Geschichte und Gegenwart*, 1st ed., Mohr, Tübingen, 1927, p. 1618.

participated in the controversy with their fists. When one entered a barber's shop, say, in Alexandria or Chalcedon, one was immediately asked: 'What do you think about the "two natures"?' The conclusive answer was given at the Council of Nicea (325) not as a result of a theological agreement, but enforced by the power of the Emperor. Constantine, aiming at a union of East and West in his realm, needed a united Church for this purpose, just as today the Kremlin has no patience with the intellectual quarrels of the many varieties of humanists, agnostics, atheists, Marxists and Marxists-Leninists, but establishes the dogma by means of purges, prison camps and other threats to human freedom. The Fathers of the Church eventually gave up the search for a final dogmatic formula and had to be satisfied with a *via media* between Judaism and Hellenism, between monotheism on the one hand and a popular polytheism on the other. Christ as *theos deuteros*, as a 'second God', remained the theological stumbling-block of the Christian monotheist.

But the success of the Church Fathers must not be overlooked. They succeeded in translating the message of the prophets and rabbis, oriental in its origin, to the Western world and from there it struck root again in the East. In comparison with this successful universalism of the Fathers of the Church the humanist of today is a provincial, conditioned by, and for, the needs of the Western technological camp. The Western humanist, who acknowledges only the Promethean nature of man and disregards the image of God in the human frame, is not yet a citizen of the One World, which will be born in suffering and travail. The One World, if it is to come, cannot be merely a world-wide manufacturing society of producers and consumers. Such a society is not a fit place for human beings. Man, created in the image of God, has needs beyond manufacturing and consuming. This is the challenge which begins to force the humanism of today either to change, or to remain a splinter movement of philosophies, doctrines and theologies which are no longer valid. The humanist is the by-product of an urban civilization which is too narrow to become world-wide. The humanist suppresses the creature of God in man and drives creative man to a frenzy without sabbath or peace. In this case he becomes what Herbert Marcuse calls 'one-dimensional man'.

One-dimensional man is crippled and affected with a sickness which must lead to the extinction of the human species. Fortunately one-dimensional man is an abstraction, created by Marxist sociology. True men of flesh and blood can lose their humanity and become the inhuman residue brought forth by a theory hostile to man, as God wished him to live.

On the whole, the humanist who is nothing but a humanist is a rare bird. In reality the humanist is still an heir who unknowingly lives on the capital of his Jewish and Christian heritage; even his Athenian past prevents the humanist from becoming one-dimensional man, man who is 'finitude closed in itself' (Tillich). Man with one 'nature', that of immanence alone, man without the 'nature' which points to transcendence beyond himself, is a theoretical proposition. No such man dwells on this earth, which is admittedly populated by too many crooks and wicked men. But Herbert Marcuse's one-dimensional man is a monster. No mother gave birth to him and no father begot him. The spectre of this monster appeared on the horizon of the sociologist, who has confused the manufacturing society of the technological age with the world created by God.

After what we have experienced in a history dominated by Hitlerism and Stalinism, it has become difficult for many people to affirm the biblical view of man according to the text 'God created man in his own image'. The title of a book published in East Berlin reads: *Man – The Miraculous Being*. But in this case the praise is not the praise of Psalm 139:14: 'I will give thanks unto Thee, for I am fearfully and wonderfully made'. The Communist author praises man who has penetrated space and thinks himself independent of the power of God.

The mystery of the human person, of his uniqueness, the mystery of the fact that no man is what his fellow-man is, the mystery of the absence of any duplication in the host of men – this is the essence of biblical anthropology. In biblical literature the name by which man is addressed, plays a decisive role. The name points to a person who is marked, but not by political or social characteristics. Environment makes numerous people appear like each other. The name indicates a person who alone has this name. The name lifts one person out of a multitude of persons as unique. In spite of all biological interconnections with his ancestors, with subsequent generations and with his relatives every man is somebody who exists only once. This is powerfully and clearly expressed in Psalm 139, which in its twenty-four verses relates the uniqueness of man to that of God, explaining the former by the latter: 'I will give thanks unto Thee, for I am fearfully and wonderfully made . . .'

Biblical anthropology becomes idolatry in a humanism without any kind of monotheistic impact. Man in whom the image of God is ignored becomes the idol of this type of humanist. Nothing else is seen above or besides man; he becomes a cypher, which, when decoded, might tally with the different explanations offered by the various schools of psychology. But it does not mean man. As man remains the creature who is by nature a worshipper, humanism cut off from monotheism becomes idolatrous worship of man.

Like Islam, humanism preserves the concept of man as it prevailed in Hellenistic antiquity. In the partial similarity between Islam and humanism there is a positive element which has to be acknowledged. Scholars of the school of comparative religion have called Islam a 'carrier of religions'. Islam often displays Jewish and Christian ideas and accepts some of their religious practices. Sometimes it contradicts Jewish and Christian tenets, sometimes it assimilates them to its own faith. Islam as a carrier of religions is involved in a constant dialogue with the other two monotheistic religions. It is the same with humanism. We find many examples where humanism contradicts Judaism and Christianity and yet at the same time it is a 'carrier' of ideas and maxims which Jew and Christian profess themselves. Marxist humanism, for instance, holds as fast to the idea of a united mankind as did any biblical prophet.

Islam and humanism display their ambiguity as 'carriers' of monotheism. There is in Islam also another ambiguity. Islam is 'Semitic Hellenism'. Islam threw off the Hellenistic way of life, but the Muslim empire-builders continued to walk in the ways of Hellenistic civilization. Something similar happens with humanism. With some humanists of our own day a European Hellenism comes to the fore. Humanism as modern European Hellenism is often paganism, noble, refined, but paganism just the same. It need not be so. A co-existence between humanism and the three monotheistic religions is possible. The possibility is easier to achieve for Judaism than for Christianity. The Book of Ecclesiastes is part of the Old Testament. This book may have had an author with leanings towards Greek thinking, but it had an editor who remained rooted in Judaism. The postscript of this Jewish editor transformed Ecclesiastes into a Jewish book. The postscripts reads: 'The end of the matter, all having been heard: fear God, and keep His commandments: for this is the whole duty of man!'

Humanism in the Renaissance rejoiced in the discovery of man. It met man first exclusively in the man of letters. In Petrarch, a humanist of the Renaissance, the Platonist is stronger than the heir to Judaeo-Christian traditions. Petrarch surrounds himself with manuscripts of Greek and Latin authors, with coins and medals of Greek and Roman antiquity and has in his study a bust of Homer in front of which he burns an oil lamp, as piously as Roman Catholics do in front of the Madonna. Mankind shrinks in the view of the humanist to a small circle, the European book-reading community. But viewed from the various ghettos of the Middle Ages – clerical, scholastic and denominational – the Renaissance was a step into fresh air, a step towards the real, the God-created world, uniting the families of mankind into one humanity.

The Christian humanist Erasmus (1466–1536) spent the years of his working life in free countries, in Holland and in Switzerland. Humanism prospers only in places where freedom is granted to man. Erasmus was always writing: books, pamphlets, letters, appeals. Honest writing, writing for the cause of truth and justice, needs freedom. Would that nobility, refinement, and readiness for peaceful dialogue had influenced the wild Martin Luther! European history would have been spared the terrors of the Thirty Years' War, if these two men had worked together. It was not to be. With his *Vale Erasme* which branded Erasmus as a heretic deserting the one cause, seen as the only true cause, Luther turned away from the humanists who wielded no power. Luther cooperated with those who had power: with the *Fürsten* (princes).

Johan Huizinga, the great historian, in his book *The Waning of the Middle Ages*, defies romantic apologetics which propose a continuation of the Middle Ages in one way or another. The Middle Ages have passed and had to pass. The humanist is in every respect a post-medieval man. To acknowledge him as such means to emancipate oneself from the Middle Ages and to progress towards the new, the coming era. But to acknowledge the humanist in his right as a man of our times need not mean that it is necessary to see him uncritically. Johan Huizinga in his 'In Commemoration of Erasmus' (see Huizinga, 1960) admires and praises his Dutch fellow-countryman. Erasmus 'had the courage not to play the hero'. But Huizinga also says of the Christian humanist Erasmus: 'It is hard for us to accept (his) piety with such a strong aesthetic tinge as serious.' 'The words of the Old Testament prophets found little echo, and those of the Psalmist solely in long-winded paraphrases.' 'Erasmus' voice hardly ever has the sound of coming *de profundis*.'

The Jewish and the Christian humanist are both identical in their difference from the intellectual scientist or the politician, who understand the universe and rule society by the exclusive application of ideas. God, not encountered in worship, but approached by speculation, becomes an idea which man can manipulate as he pleases. This is the point at which the humanist becomes an ideocrat. He becomes the demonic intellectual who is obsessed. He is obsessed with only one of Plato's three ideas: of the good, the true, the beautiful. These three ideas dominate Plato's city, of which even the modern humanist is still a citizen. Not so the intellectual who has to be understood as an ideocrat. The ideocrat is demonic man who builds the totalitarian society, be it as scientist or as politician. His ancestor is not Plato, who believed his ideas of the good, the true and the beautiful to be deeply rooted in the ground of which the orphic mystics spoke, as the prophets spoke of their revelations. The ancestors of the ideocrat can be seen in Hegel. Today Hegel is alive in the Marxist. From one absolute idea the particulars are evolved. In the tyranny which enslaves man the highest idea and the various regulative ideas construct a monolithic society. Herbert Marcuse standing on the beach in Santa Barbara and facing the wide and turbulent ocean reacted in a way which his critic and biographer Habermas recorded in the words: '*Wie kann es da immer noch Leute geben, die die Existenz von Ideen leugnen* (And yet there are people who still deny the existence of ideas)!' In moments of deep emotion Herbert Marcuse speaks German. He is an American who is a German under his skin just like Werner von Braun. Every normal person facing the thundering waves of the ocean and its wide horizon would have responded by thinking of the frailty and futility of man-made ideas. Job, pondering over the power which the ocean revealed to him, was brought back to his God by the experience of nature's display of the *mysterium tremendum et fascinosum*. The intellectual allows the universe to shrink to a size which man's idea can map out. His deification of man is preceded by a reduction of man to his cerebral function: man is deprived of his divine nature, and God is dethroned.

The indictment of the intellectual, when he is an ideocrat, does not apply to the humanist. George Steiner writes in *Language and Silence* (1967, p. 81): 'The humanities do not humanize.' This statement is a false approach to the humanities. They consist of science, ethics and aesthetics, all of which are equally important. Disorder sets in only when one of the constituents is omitted or its influence diminished to the detriment of the other two. If the scientist disregards ethics or aesthetics he becomes the ideocrat of whom we spoke. He becomes the technocrat responsible for pollution and for the transformation of God's world into an asphalt desert and, worse, for the bomb. We must, therefore, insist on a moratorium on production, and urge Promethean man to learn humility.

If morality is disregarded in Plato's trinity of science, ethics and aesthetics, barbarism is at our gates. If art is the only element in man's life, he eventually becomes the spineless connoisseur moving from one aesthetic impression to the next; he exists from one bottle to the other, drinking *lethe*, the waters of oblivion, to forget what he is, when he is himself. The three elements of the humanities can truly guide man, but all three must guide him in unison. In addition and above all, man must also stand before the burning bush and, as did Moses, hear the message: 'I AM: that is who I am' (Exod. 3:14). If he does not listen to this message which makes monotheism the great message of hope, the humanist is an exponent of that polytheistic trinity which the Church Fathers undertook to change in their gigantic mental struggle with Plato and Aristotle. The aim of these Christian giants of philosophical thinking was to replace the philosophical polytheistic trinity by Hebrew monotheism. Their fight was no longer against the polytheism of a naively believing populace. The gods of Homer were dead. Their fight was against the polytheism of the Hellenistic intellectual. The modern humanist is not a polytheist, he confesses a philosophically conceived trinity. He believes in science, ethics and art, the trinity of autonomous man. But he believes. To quote I Corinthians 11:19 again: 'Heresies there must be.' The heretic can force those whom he has left to think again and thereby to find the strength necessary for revival. The humanist is the heretic who can, if changed, himself help to strengthen monotheism.

The humanities *do* humanize; they civilize. The humanist is a child of a civilization deserving to be called human civilization. But civilization is exposed to the rhythm of rise and fall. Steiner, in his desperate phrase 'the humanities do not humanize', suffers from the traumatic experience of all the millions who remember Hitler. When barbarism is at the gates, the humanist is a feeble defender. With the torturing vision of the decay of the Austro-Hungarian Empire the Austrian poet Grillparzer uttered the warning: 'From humanism to nationalism and from nationalism to barbarism.' The barbarism which extinguished 'the lights all over Europe' did not break into Germany out of the Asian steppes. The barbarism in our midst is the danger. The domestication of the barbarian is an undertaking whose success is questionable. Domestication is not enough. A cannibal who eats with a knife and fork is still a cannibal. It is not domestication but conversion which is needed. To convert the barbarian is possible, as two thousand years of Christian history have proved to some degree. The dark hours which Europe experienced under the heel of Hitler are directly the consequence of a breakdown of Christianity and are only indirectly the fault of humanism, only in so far as humanism is (though as a heresy) a part of Christianity. The Christian spiritual infusion into the society of man, the Jewish sanctification of the profane ways of man, transform this vulnerable civilization into a fortress, which the barbarian cannot conquer. The process 'from humanism to nationalism, from nationalism to barbarism' is inevitable only where history does not transcend man; man is reduced to being immanent in himself alone, because he is only one nature and not also that other nature, in which he is the image of God. Anchored in the transcendence of God man is not threatened by an inevitable law. He enjoys freedom.

More than a decade before Bonhoeffer coined the term 'religionless Christianity', Rosenzweig too expressed his negative attitude to the term 'religion' (see page 80). Lately the theological writings of Leo Baeck, whose memory German Jews rightly revere as that of a saint, have been closely scrutinized. The Roman Catholic theologians, E. Przywara and H. U. von Balthasar, say in so many words: this is all humanism and not what is to be expected from the preacher of a monotheistic faith! An author is mirrored in the book which he has written, but he is never identical with it. From Mendelssohn to Leo Baeck German Jews as men of letters were part of that humanist culture which flourished in Germany as nowhere else. Humanism helped the German Jews to leave their Middle Ages and yet remain faithful Jews. We still live in the revolution which started in 1789. In the age from Marx to Trotsky, German Jews sent their sons to help the cause of progress. This help was forthcoming in the universities and laboratories and on the barricades. German Jews entered Christian Europe not as trinitarians, but as Jewish heretical binitarians. They believed in a Holy Ghost, the spirit of the poets and thinkers and they believed in a Christology different from the dogma of the Church, yet not different from the message of the Suffering Servant of Isaiah 53. The two young Jews Gustav Landauer and Eugen Levine who were murdered by White Terror in 1919 in Munich were laying down their lives in express knowledge of their sacrificial death. The death on the Cross, as the narrative of the Gospels describes it, was before their eyes when they went to their death. Jewish humanists shed their aesthetic frame of mind. As servants of the age to come they made their sacrifice in work, blood and tears. The Jewish humanists of German Jewry combined a messianic faith with their humanism.

After his return from Theresienstadt Leo Baeck said to me: 'Read the Book of Daniel!' In the Book of Daniel Jewish messianism, though remaining the messianism of the prophets, becomes eschatological messianism. 'Go thou thy way till the end be . . .' (Dan. 12:13). Messianism serves mankind, serves history, leading to the goal promised by God. God 'changeth the times and seasons: he removeth kings and setteth up kings' (Dan. 2:21). God's goal for history is the kingdom of justice, truth and mercy. But in his most private existence man is concerned with last things: guilt, atonement and death. In history man is a willing or a disobedient fellow-traveller of God. The humanist may have his good record as messianic man. Let him read the Book of Daniel, where he is bidden to 'move hopefully towards the end'. The humanist must do what he has not done so far; he is still outside the monotheistic camp. He must learn to join those who are constituted as a society not only by messianic hope but also by eschatological hope. He must learn to worship God; in doing so the humanist ceases to be a humanist and has arrived at the place from which he came. The humanist never was and never is far from God. God is God. He will not be apprehended by anything and anybody. He is free to reveal Himself in His glory and in His impenetrable silence and is also free to permit only one single image of Himself: man.

DEATH AND THE HUMANIST

'and now it comes, the point of all points, . . .'
(from Rosenzweig's last letter to Buber. He
died before he could finish it.)

The difference between all preceding philosophies and the 'New Thinking' has consequences for the understanding of man. Hermann Cohen and Rosenzweig, following his old master, moved away from the concept of creative man towards the concept of man, the creature. Man, who understands himself as a created being, has transcended the finiteness which man in his pride as creator has ignored. All the creations of man, summarized in what the Germans solemnly call *Kultur*, culture, collapse like a house of cards when the storm of history blows. In *The Star of Redemption* Rosenzweig does justice to man's endeavour of mirroring eternity by creating culture, but he is also an outspoken critic of the vanity fair of a culture which decays into play. The right of Jewish culture to be called Jewish is questioned. We have the Hebrew word *avodah* which means both 'work' and 'worship'. For the justification of culture we would need a Hebrew word meaning 'culture'. Biblical Hebrew does not provide such a word. The Israeli Hebrew word for culture is as new as the Israeli Hebrew word for electricity. Modern man without God gives culture that glory Plato and Hegel gave to their eternal ideas (Maybaum, 1960, pp. 46–82; 1969, pp. 153–5).

Rosenzweig's criticism sprang from the mood of all those who realized that World War I had shattered the security which man as creator imagined he received from civilization. When *The Star of Redemption* appeared, this publication was recognized as one of the 'war books' which authors wrote out of the experience of trench warfare. The expectation of survival of a soldier at the Somme was three weeks. Civilization could afford man no protection. His place in the created world had to be humbly admitted. With the two facts Man and World the third fact, God, appeared as the subject-matter of 'The New Thinking'. A new humanism, a humanism not without but with God, a Jewish humanism, became visible. Rosenzweig called it 'absolute empiricism'. As World and Man are given facts in themselves, God is a given fact in the experience of man. Rosenzweig spoke of the 'logic of creation', a concept which he took from Schelling. With this element of Schelling as his philosophical starting-point Rosenzweig emancipated himself from Hegel. The opponent still follows the opposed master. Humanists of the Marxist brand are the late satellites of Hegel, who saw man as man the creator, as part of the *Geist*, the spirit. Hegel is the last philosopher of the Pauline pattern, applying the dichotomy of body and spirit to man. When man dies, Hegel and Paul have no message for the body that dies while his soul flies away into the realm of the spirit. Man is in this way betrayed, his encounter with death remains the life-long fear that nothing but the end in the grave awaits him. The humanist philosophy, being without an answer to death, is the old philosophy which Rosenzweig overcomes by his 'New Thinking'. Rosenzweig writes: 'when Life has closed its eloquent lips, he (Death) will open his eternally silent mouth and say: "Do you recognize me? I am your brother" ' (Glatzer, 1953, p. 213). In writing this, Rosenzweig is not a humanist. He may be called a Jewish humanist, who thinks and speaks to us like the writers of the Hebrew Bible.

With the step from man the creator to man the creature, from humanism without God to a humanism with God, a new theology has to be considered. The first part of *The Star of Redemption* has the motto: 'In *philosophos*!', the second: 'In *theologos*!' Rosenzweig wants to be both, philosopher and theologian.

> In order to rid itself of clichés, indeed for the sake of its very status as science, philosophy today requires 'theologians' to philosophize – theologians, however, now likewise in a new sense. For as will now be seen, the theologian whom philosophy requires for the sake of its scientific status is himself a theologian who requires philosophy – for the sake of his integrity . . . (*Star*, p. 106).

The subject of this philosophical theology or, say, theological philosophy is not an 'I', which is an abstraction, but a real person. Rosenzweig explains passionately: I in my private existence, I, with my first and my second name want to philosophize. I want to know not this or that, but I want to know the one thing which really matters. Man who is hungry, who is happy or unhappy, bored or fascinated, this real man must become the subject matter of philosophy. What happens to me, to my individual existence? Hegel, representing the 'old philosophy', the philosophy from Thales to himself, has a curious answer. 'Only' the individual dies. But in the *All* (the Whole), in this nebulous abstraction in which God, man and world are summed up, nothing dies.

In this way the man who asks questions about his individual existence is cheated. His individual existence disappears into the generalities of the philosophy of history. This is the essence of Hegel's idealistic philosophy, the German philosophy, in which those who call themselves humanists in the English-speaking, and therefore English-thinking, world follow their German masters without much thought. This is the philosophy against which Rosenzweig fought in his 'New Thinking'. Hegel teaches: we do not die into the dust, we do not die into God, we die into the 'Whole' (*das All*), into this fabrication of German historical idealism. Thus history becomes the Moloch devouring hecatombs. The way of German idealism leads from Hegel to Hitler. What makes man the creature who can only blush when calling himself creator is the knowledge of the inevitability of his death. This knowledge man cannot and must not forget.

Rosenzweig was not the man to forget it. We have the following note by his friend Hermann Badt, who visited the student Rosenzweig in May 1908, that is long before Rosenzweig became engaged in philosophical writing:

> I came early in the morning and found Franz still in bed. I was permitted to witness the levée and teased him about the length of time it took him and the almost ritualistic ceremonial with which he surrounded it. He reacted to this by giving a long lecture that was half-serious, half in fun. Indeed, he said, the moment of daily reawakening from nightly death was for him the greatest and holiest moment of the day. It was impossible ever to dwell too fondly on this daily renewal, one must taste it consciously in every detail. On that occasion, if I remember rightly, he first spoke those words which he was to repeat later under different circumstances, and which gave me much food for thought. He said that he alone is truly blessed

who is able not only to experience consciously this daily reawakening but also in the moment of death to remain conscious and make the step from this world to the next with his senses still intact (Glatzer, 1953, p. 17).

An old rabbi could have expressed the same thoughts as the twenty-two-year-old youth. But this youth was Rosenzweig who, years later, called the first chapter of his *Star of Redemption* 'Concerning Death' (pp. 3–5). Here he warns against the mere philosophical consolation in the face of death. This old philosophy from the Stoa to Hegel is 'cruel lying' (p. 5) to man who is always and naturally afraid of death. But death is swallowed up in eternal triumph (Isa. 25:8) in the new philosophy in which Rosenzweig pleads for a concept of life in which death is not an end, but a part of life. 'Where does the way lead?' asks Rosenzweig at the end of the *Star*. His answer, valid also at the grave side, is: into life. The great commandment 'Love your neighbour as yourself' can be truly fulfilled where the 'neighbour' is approached in awe and with the knowledge that he is on his way to death. The day of death is everyman's great day of atonement; death atones for everything; death leads into peace.

> To walk humbly with thy God – nothing more is demanded there than a wholly present trust. But trust is a big word. It is the seed whence grow faith, hope, and love and the fruit which ripens out of them. It is the very simplest and just for that the most difficult. . . . To walk humbly with thy God – the words are written over the gate, the gate which leads out of the mysterious-miraculous light of the divine sanctuary in which no man can remain alive. Whither, then, do the wings of the gate open? Thou knowest it not? INTO LIFE (*Star*, p. 424).

MAN – 'LITTLE LOWER THAN THE ANGELS . . .' (Ps. 8:6)

Gotthold Ephraim Lessing, the friend of Moses Mendelssohn, writes in his play *Nathan the Wise*: 'It suffices to be a man.' Wherever the sun of the West penetrated history and created civilized human life this doctrine concerning man was affirmed. With Lessing and Mendelssohn this doctrine remained theistic humanism: man did not dethrone God, God revealed himself in man, created in His image. For Lessing and Mendelssohn man was not merely an abstract concept which did not reveal anything of the miraculous realities which made man what he was. But even the abstract concept of man propagated by the philosophy of Enlightenment became the trumpet sound announcing the end of the Middle Ages. The chorus of Beethoven's Ninth Symphony, 'Be embraced, ye millions', greeted the New Era. For the time being, it was prudent not to be too radical. The Eastern European disciples of Mendelssohn gave the advice: 'Be a Jew in your home, and a man outside it.' The man who is a Jew need not be a hero, but he is able to become one; he need not be a saint, but is able to be one. He does not make history, but eternally populates history. He is eternal, whereas history remains a succession of episodes.

It suffices to be a man, man worshipping God, loving his neighbour, wrestling with sin and desiring atonement. In their anthropology Lessing and, even more, Mendelssohn were guided by reason, not by historical research. 'History bores me', said Mendelssohn. In history we meet Jew, Christian, Muslim – and Buddhist. With the awakening of Asia a fourth type has stepped forward confronting the European trinity. The Jew alone can remain a Jew and accept the commandment 'be a man', a man who, as a man, is faithful to God. The Christian is, as indicated by the phrase 'second Adam', a changed man. The Muslim too, in his obedience to God, as a 'slave of God', is no longer in the position to say 'It suffices to be a man', and the Buddhist has, in the suppression of all desires, ceased to be a man, as he enters this world. The great gift to mankind, the doctrine 'It suffices to be a man', has been accepted by the Jew outside and independent of the Enlightenment movement. The prophets and teachers of the Hebrew Bible understand man, whether righteous or sinful, whether prophet or layman, in life and in death, as inseparable from God. Man can never run away from God, as Jonah tried to do. God reached him even in the belly of the whale.

Biblical man understands himself as this kind of man, as man who is a creature of God. It suffices to be man. The post-medieval Jew, still speaking his German-Yiddish, understands the commandment 'Be a *Mensch*' (Be human) as a God-given commandment. In this formulation the Jew is not man of the Enlightenment. The commandment 'Be a man' means: be what everybody else is, or be a hero, eventually be a superman. All these meanings are excluded in the Yiddish version: Be a *Mensch*. In this version the commandment means, be what God wants man to be.

The European Enlightenment is a movement in which peace is proclaimed between Jew and Christian. The friendship between Lessing and Mendelssohn is symbolic of this happy period. The period of romanticism brings the Christian onto the stage, and he becomes again, as he has been all through Christian history, hostile to the Jew. The most successful propagator of the Enlightenment movement is the philosopher, Voltaire's *philosophe*. He looks forward hopefully to a future which will be better than the past. The mouthpiece of the romantic movement is the poet, who nostalgically in aesthetic contemplation, yearns for the civilization of the past. Reality became an imagined, a spiritualized, and therefore a distorted reality. The romantic period had one important, unexpected consequence: It brought the historian, often no less a revolutionary figure than the philosopher, onto the stage. The past was studied, and light was shed on what tradition had left in uncritical reverence. The past ceased to be the dark, unknown past. The first contribution to a better Christian understanding of Jews and Judaism was the rehabilitation of the Pharisees by the historian. Jesus, if he ever lived, was a Pharisee or belonged to one of the sects aligned in partial agreement with the Pharisees.

The decisive contribution of the historian was rendered in Biblical criticism. Biblical criticism initiated the post-Christian era, in which Christianity is left without a historical Jesus. There is a parallel in modern Judaism. The Torah, the Gospels, the Koran, are literature. They were written and have to be studied like the works of Shakespeare and Goethe, Plato and Kant and other great writers. The historian has robbed man of the belief that literature can offer absolute truth. It can only offer relative truth, truth scrutinized by criticism and subjected to constantly changing interpretation. Besides God there is only one who is unchanging in the ever-changing history of man, and that is man. What we know about truth, love, justice, hope, we know from man. Books become dated, the human heart is the eternal place where God speaks to man.

If it suffices to be a man – a view accepted by the Jew – why be a Jew? The Jew establishes his separate social existence, making a federation of Jewish families his religious home. Where a family is established, God is present. The Jew desires to be 'the people dwelling alone'. But his aim is to have in the particular community of Jewish families a 'firstfruit' of what a united mankind will be at the end of days. The messianic universalist dream of a united mankind and the intimacy of the separated particular group are not opposites in Jewish social life. The Jewish people upholds a unity which is similar to that which makes a nation a solid group. But the Jewish people is not a nation. As a Jew the Jew remains a man, a truly human person. In the nation the humanity of man is curtailed, man is in various ways sacrificed to the needs of the nation. However much the age of nationalism, now coming to an end through the rise of super-powers, has forced Jews to become like the gentiles, we must hold fast to what it means to be a Jew. It means to be a man. However great the glory of the Israeli soldier may be – it is great indeed through his saving Israelis from genocide at the hands of the Arabs – let us not forget the glory of man who is progenitor of everything God wants him to be and to do. Man, who is a Jew, is also the progenitor of the Christian and the Muslim.

The idea that Christianity and Islam have their root in Judaism is expressed in Judah ha-Levi's parable of the seed and the tree with the two branches: Christianity and Islam. Franz Rosenzweig loved to refer approvingly to this parable. It is a sign of the epoch-making change severing the Middle Ages from our new era that this parable, which was previously well suited to express the relationship between the three monotheistic religions, has now to be critically approached and amended. The seed knows nothing of the tree. This is one point which makes Judah ha-Levi's parable no longer satisfactory. The second point is that the metaphor does not express any responsibility of the seed for the tree.

The medieval Jew knew nothing of Christianity. To him Christians were gentiles and gentiles only. 'The Jew walks through history without a sideward glance.' This was the admirable medieval attitude of the Jew. It can no longer be upheld. Today the Jew walks at the side of the Christian. The Jewish child grows up with Christian children and mixes with them in the playground and at school. When Jewish children learn English poems they are taught Christianity. Today in the West, the Jew has a great deal of knowledge concerning Christianity. Judah ha-Levi's parable of the seed lacks any reference to this fact.

Nor does this parable stipulate any Jewish responsibility for the Christian and the Muslim. Nor is the responsibility of Christian and Muslim for the Jew included in the parable. A seed–tree relationship takes place in nature, and nature is mute. Jew, Christian and Muslim stand in history, in which the muteness of nature must be overcome by man communicating with man. In our new era Jew, Christian and Muslim speak with each other. There is a trialogue between them, and this trialogue brings the Middle Ages to an end. It is no longer enough to say that Christianity and Islam 'grow' out of the seed of Judaism. They do, but do they always grow in the right way and in the right direction? Is the tree always the plant that we expect to grow from the seed, or does the seed produce unwanted shoots, possible heresies? Most important is the question: have the branches, Christianity and Islam, always the benefit of the sap which comes from Judaism? Is it not sometimes more a Greek, or for that matter a German, plant which has, in perversion of its origin, grown from the Jewish seed? In the modern era, that is in the post-medieval era, Jews cannot but willingly accept responsibility for what happens in Christianity and Islam. The Christian needs the Jew at his side. The Jew does not view the world in the way of Greek cerebral, conceptual thought. All people have acquired a scientific view of the world, dustmen as well as professional scientists. They all have become Greeks. The antagonism Greek–Jew is today with us, as it was in the past. The Christian needs to have at his side the man who is not a Greek. He needs the Jew. So does the Muslim. The Jew, though he may still be a Semite, is not a fatalist. The Jew can demonstrate to the Muslim an obedience which is offered in freedom. Close correlation between Jew, Christian and Muslim on the stage of history enacts the *Divina Commedia* in which each of these three members of the monotheistic family walks on his way to God. Without this correlation a situation besets history in which the Jew is not a Jew, the Christian not a Christian, the Muslim not a Muslim. Jews who are truly Jews, Christians who are truly Christians and Muslims who are truly Muslims are all over the world that united community which can in the end successfully save mankind from Asiatic mysticism and from nihilism driving man into an oblivion of his self, into Nirvana, and a use of rituals, philosophy and drugs for the destruction of the humanity of man.

A Christian sculptor put at the entry of Strasbourg Cathedral two women, one, blindfold, representing the defeated Synagogue, the other depicting the victorious Church. As a sign of her defeat the Synagogue has at her side a broken staff fallen to the ground, the Church, on the other hand, was given by the artist the semblance of majesty and absolute rule. As Judah ha-Levi's parable of the seed and the tree only has meaning in the Middle Ages and no longer represents the post-medieval situation, so it is with the work of this Christian sculptor. In the Middle Ages the Synagogue lived in the ghetto enforced on the Jews by the Church. According to the Christian Church the Synagogue was despised and yet tolerated, Christ was a Jew, but the Jews, once chosen, had lost their privileges. As a blindfolded woman the Synagogue cannot see what goes on around her. But her blindness in the present does not prevent her from gazing into the future and in this way upholding her prophetic role. The sculptor was not without justice to the Synagogue. Some art critics even find that he gave the Synagogue a spiritual beauty and let the Church, on the other hand, appear in the harshness of a cold ruler. However that may be, the medieval concept of the relationship between Synagogue and Church no longer describes our post-medieval situation. The Church is no longer the militant Church. The Constantinian bond between Church and Empire has come to an end, and the Synagogue is no longer, if it ever was, silent, that is, without the eye-opening power of doctrines. The medieval artist put her, blindfold, beside the Church, who in powerful majesty was revered as the institution instructing mankind with the help of her dogma. Since Mendelssohn, Jews in the West are able to express their faith in doctrine, ideology and philosophy, working out the answer to the question: what is Judaism? Standing in the Christian world the emancipated Jew has responded to Christian dogma with various modern Jewish theories about the 'essence of Judaism'. Not through law alone, but through theory and doctrine the post-medieval Jew makes his once silent existence articulate. Franz Rosenzweig still cherished the sculpture of the blindfolded woman with the broken staff and regarded it as an apt representation of Jewish existence. Existence is mute, doctrine speaks, but existence is deeper, richer in meaning than doctrine. This much can be conceded to Rosenzweig. But since the emancipation of the Jews through the Enlightenment movement, the silent side-by-side existence of Jew and Christian belongs to the past. The Jew can no longer withdraw behind the fence of an indisputable Law. The Jew must speak. And the Christian, who has discovered the Jew with his still valid election, must listen.

A Protestant professor of theology once tried to convince Hermann Cohen that faith in God has, through the added faith in Christ, a warmth which is missing in the monotheism of the Old Testament. 'What,' answered Cohen, 'the Lord is my shepherd, I shall want nothing!' Cohen told Franz Rosenzweig of this answer, in which he defended his uncompromising monotheism against the Christian theologian with the words of Psalm 23. 'I can still hear today,' writes Rosenzweig, 'the thundering grumble "What", the silent accent on the words "the Lord" and the triumphant conclusion, thrust out like one single word "I shall want nothing".' Franz Rosenzweig recorded other passionate exclamations of Cohen in defence of Jewish monotheism. 'God be what He be, but He must be One ... On this point we cannot come to an understanding with Christianity.' 'The unity of God, this most abstract idea ... for whose sake we are killed all the day' (Cohen quotes here Psalm 44:23: 'Because of Thee we are done to death all day long and treated as sheep for slaughter'). 'The Greek spirit, that is, the scientific mind, looks for mediation, as they call it, between God and man. To this Greek charm the Jew Philo and his Logos fell victim.' 'Had Philo not invented the Logos, no Jew would ever have fallen away from God.' We can amplify this last sentence with the thought: had the Jew Philo not introduced the concept of Logos to some groups of hellenized Jews, no Christian would have made his appearance in the world.

Cohen passionately upheld the religio-political consequences of the affirmation of the oneness of God. State or nation or culture are splendid attractions for man whose loyalty to them is like the loyalty to a 'second God'. The 'most abstract idea' of the One God, on the other hand, is correlated to the concept of the One People. 'Balaam's word of the "people that shall dwell alone" [Num. 23:9], the civilized world cannot comprehend it', sighs Cohen. Can the Israeli, who has now entered political history and plays this game so successfully, comprehend it? Can Israelis agree with Franz Rosenzweig, who, in harmony with Balaam's understanding of the Jewish people, could still say: 'The Jew wanders through history without a sideward glance'? The Israeli must glance carefully at every move from Cairo, Amman, Moscow and Washington. Israel must respond carefully, diplomatically and culturally, and cannot afford to be the 'people that shall dwell alone'. She is like the gentiles in the midst of history and, like the gentiles, shaped not by the One God but by history, by the Logos. But in the beginning was not the Logos, in the beginning was, is and will remain, God 'and nothing besides him'.

Franz Rosenzweig found Cohen an uncompromising Jew who insisted on the fundamental difference between Judaism and Christianity. Cohen was at the time of his influence on Rosenzweig an old man who had a life of fame as a Kantian philosopher behind him. But in his lectures at the *Lehranstalt* in 1913–14 of which Rosenzweig said 'my happy ears were privileged to listen', Cohen rebelled against Plato and Kant and returned 'from the world' 'to his people'. But we would do well also to consider his earlier views. He was always a committed Jew, faithful to the world of his father who was a teacher in a small Jewish community in Germany. Young Cohen discussed his entry into Marburg University, which he was destined to raise to a centre of German philosophy with the then Principal Albert Lange, the author of *The History of Materialism*. Lange said to the young applicant: 'About Christianity we cannot talk.' Cohen's reply was: 'Very well, what you call Christianity, I call prophetic Judaism.' In this young Cohen was mistaken, and he corrected his mistake in his later confession: 'My Judaism is the Judaism of the Prophets *and* Pharisees.' The ambiguous term 'prophetic Judaism', in itself an appropriate attribute of Judaism at all periods of Jewish history, gave rise to what I may term nineteenth-century 'Christology', which spoke of Jesus and Amos as social reformers, even as socialists. At the time of Renan, Schweitzer and other liberal Christians Jesus was spoken of in a way which was not acceptable to orthodox Christianity and which could mislead Jews to give up their absolute rejection of Jesus.

Jesus has no place in the world of the Jew. The nineteenth-century 'Christology' proclaimed Jesus the Reformer, the Revolutionary, Jesus the Socialist, Jesus Isaiah's Servant of God, Jesus the true Jewish heir of the prophets. This shallow Christology had its Jewish and Christian authors who in each case misunderstood both Judaism and Christianity. The American rabbi Eisendrath addressed a meeting of Christians with the passionate demand: 'Give us back our Jesus!', the Viennese historian Friedrich Heer, lecturing at the London Institute of Jewish Affairs, prophesied: Jesus comes home to his people. Both Hermann Cohen and Franz Rosenzweig are important opponents of nineteenth-century Christology. There is a difference between the two. Cohen stops at his Jewish radical monotheism; Rosenzweig, remaining a disciple of Cohen, looks beyond the unbridgeable gap between Judaism and Christianity and sees a possibility of two ways to God – the Jewish and the Christian. But he is blind to Islam as a third way to God.

Cohen is admirable as the 'stubborn' Jew rejecting a possible Jewish understanding of Christianity. 'Jesus Christ – a god, never has any man believed it', whispered the old man with a shudder. He brushed aside two thousand years of Christianity and the subtleties of the Church Fathers, who reconciled monotheism with the dogma of the Trinity, the Reformation and the modern Christology of the nineteenth century. Against all these dogmatic attempts at reconciliation Cohen did not only say that they meant nothing to him. He said more. All these millions who had lived and died with their faith in Christ have – according to Cohen – in fact doubted what they expressed to be their faith. If such a denial of Christian faith could be expressed at all in our own time, we cannot help asking: where is there today, be it among Jews or Christians, anybody who would either affirm that Cohen's denial of the godhead of Jesus is the true expression of biblical monotheism, or reject it as blasphemy? The theology of Barth, Bultmann and Bonhoeffer brings up nothing convincing from German 'depth'. Their modern, that is post-medieval, scholasticism, a tower of abstract concepts, is not the equal of Jewish God-affirming realism. A mind trained and shaped by the Hebrew Bible will not apprehend medieval or post-medieval scholasticism. God and Spirit, the Jew and Philo, the Jewish people and the gentiles, the word of a prophet and the demand of historic necessity – these are two and can never become one. One thing is certain: Christians today will have to listen to Jews and learn from their Scriptures. Jews cannot but agree with Cohen, who merely says what Jews have always said throughout the millennia of their history, although the rabbis did acknowledge the existence of the 'righteous among the nations of the world'.

With his 'Hear, O Israel . . . God is One . . . You shall love the Lord your God with your whole heart . . .' the Jew steps outside history. History has its noble aims, its programme of justice and mercy, and is not decried by the Jew as a vale which it is better to leave than to walk in. But, says Cohen, when the love of God enters a human heart, there is no room for anything else. The story of the binding of Isaac is the commentary to the 'God is One'. Does the Oneness of God give what human hearts desire, or does the Oneness of God make us ascetic despisers of anything but God? God does not demand the death of Isaac. Jewish radical monotheism makes the good life the happy goal of man. It gives the humanity of man wide scope. Whatever happiness Christianity can provide for the Christian is derived from the Judaism which permeates it. Sacrifice is the holy gift of man to God. But the way to God is possible without any ransom, without sacrifice. In the story of the binding of Isaac Isaac is not sacrificed. In the Christian interpretation Isaac is. Jesus is the sacrificed Isaac. The Jewish voice, the voice from heaven: 'Lay not thy hand upon the lad, neither do thou anything unto him' is not heard by the Christian when he cuts himself off from Judaism. The Jew is man as God created him, and man is able to move from love to justice. The Jew does not even understand, let alone accept, the need to speak to God as to two separate persons, as God of love and as God of justice. God is One.

The Hellenistic world, the West, responded to the biblical 'God is One' with the doctrine of the Trinity. To most Jews this doctrine is 'incomprehensible' (Sandmel, 1965, p. 44), but the philosophy of Plato or of Kant is also incomprehensible to many Jews. The doctrine of the Trinity has to be studied like the philosophy of Plato and Kant, and must not be neglected by Jewish scholars. If the trinity of God, history and the human mind is studied, the Jewish and the Christian scholar will give their different answers. The formula 'Father, Son and Holy Ghost', regarded by the devout medieval Christian as denoting an inexplicable mystery, has its preceding history, in which the Fathers of the early Church were not merely devout pietists, but proved to be thinkers engaged in a gigantic mental struggle. The philosophy within the doctrine of the Trinity is, like a Gothic cathedral, an admirable monument of medieval piety.

The East, Islam, confessed its monotheism in the doctrine: God is God. Rosenzweig called the formula 'God is God' a mere tautology and he therefore refused to acknowledge Islam as monotheism. Here Rosenzweig is mistaken. This resolute 'God is God' cuts short all further discussions. This treatment might often prove successful when sophisticated doubters, agnostics, humanists or scientists ask: 'God – who is he?' Islam is a very manly faith. In comparison with it, Pauline faith appears very womanly in its insistence on love as the always immediate response in the believing soul. The Muslim accepts God as reality in unsophisticated obedience. God is God – this is a powerful statement. Yet the difference between 'God is One' and 'God is God' is important. The verb 'is' in 'God is One' opens the door to further knowledge proceeding from God, not scientific but prophetic knowledge. God *is* just, merciful, forgiving sin, granting atonement. Again and again the prophet draws in exhaustive knowledge about God's being and will. The formula 'God is God' is apt for Islam, which teaches the end of prophecy. Islam is monotheism, but it is not prophetic faith. To consider that the question 'What does God demand from me?' can be answered without any reference to the written law is forbidden to the Muslim. His obedience to God is profound piety, but it is a piety without personal freedom, without the response of man's free conscience. God is God. The monotheism of the Muslim is – one is tempted to say – simple, but it is robust, powerful, uncompromising, and scorns the very idea of dispelling doubt by argument. There is a streak of Islam in the orthodoxies of Judaism and Christianity.

HUMAN – HOLY – SPIRITUAL

At the circumcision ceremony part of the prayer for the new-born boy is taken from Ezekiel. It reads: 'And I passed by you, and I saw you kicking helplessly in your own blood; and I spoke to you, there in your blood, and bade you: In your blood live!' (16:6). This is the beginning of the offspring of Zion, of the woman who represents the Jewish people, its Temple, its state, its civilization. The beginning is an utterly human situation.

Can we hope to get from Ezekiel, or, for that matter, from any writer of the Tenach, an understanding of what the Christian means when he uses the word 'spiritual', the word 'spirit', the word *pneuma*? Ezekiel and the other writers of the Hebrew Bible speak of holiness. True, the word 'holy spirit of God' is familiar to us Jews. But no Old Testament text helps us Jews to bring the Christian concept of spirit into line with Jewish thinking and Jewish evaluation. Ezekiel's 'In your blood live!' is a helpful kind of *theologia negativa*. Is the prophet thinking of spiritual guidance or spiritual hope or of a spiritual remedy to be offered to man? The answer seems to be 'no'. The prophet says to Zion: 'In your blood live!' There is no racial connotation in Ezekiel's words. Blood, in the formula 'flesh and blood', is the Hebrew phrase expressing the human situation. 'In your blood live!' means: 'be human'. In your human situation you can start out, and walking on you will find God, you will return to God and will rejoice in his nearness. Man turning to a spiritual world, be he a saint or an artist, is not human, he is involved in a super-human endeavour. He is not man but superman.

At the time of the destruction of Jerusalem, in the dark hour of the destruction of everything which history had once bestowed on the 'virgin Israel', when the gifts which culture had showered on her were taken away from her, the mere *humanum* was recognized as the ever-present beginning, offering a new start. This recognition was the great consolation in the moment of catastrophe. The prophet saw God as the passionate passer-by pointing towards the power which would let new life spring up again.

Tell her (Jerusalem) that these are the words of the Lord God to her: Canaan is the land of your ancestry and there you were born; an Amorite was your father and a Hittite your mother. This is how you were treated at birth: when you were born, your navel-string was not tied, you were not bathed in water ready for the rubbing, you were not salted as you should have been or wrapped in swaddling clothes. No one cared for you enough to do any of these things, or, indeed, to have any pity for you; you were thrown out on the bare ground in your filth on the day of your birth. Then I passed by you and saw you kicking helplessly in your own blood; and I spoke to you: In your blood live (Ezek. 16:3–6).

We read here of a situation described in a realism which may seem crude to a westerner. The oriental has no reticence in such matters. Nor has any Freudian.

The words 'In your blood live', still chanted in every circumcision service, are a proclamation of hope. Civilizations change, states crumble and disappear. Nations lead a precarious life. But the *humanum* in man's existence is permanent, is indeed eternal.

In the Middle Ages, since the ninth century a Jew was born into Islamic culture. With the arrival of Western culture, that is since Mendelssohn, a Jew has been born into different surroundings. During the last hundred and fifty years a Jew has either been born into Western or oriental culture. Yet we must not overlook the truth of the sentence 'the Jew is born a Jew'. The truth becomes visible when we compare Jew and Christian. After the first *churban*, the first holocaust, Ezekiel did not say what the Gospels said after the second *churban*, after the destruction of the Temple by the Romans. They said to the members of the Christian brotherhood: rise to the transcendent, to the spiritual height. Ezekiel said to his people: In your blood live, face the human predicament. The sanctuary in which you will worship in the diaspora is not what the Temple was. It will be, if the rabbinic translation is right, a 'little sanctuary' (11:16); it will not be a creation of an established religion, it will be a synagogue. In the mighty temples of Babylon, on the other hand, the creative mind of their architects, artists and priests had an outlet.

The Christian is not born a Christian, he becomes one. He becomes a Christian not by birth, but by a 'second birth', by the rise from the human to the spiritual status. Any person experiences a change when he becomes a citizen of a state, a member of a cult, the product of a civilization. In all these cases man, begotten by a father and born of a mother, is changed. Cult, nation, state, civilization shape man according to their image. Man transformed by an image of history has ceased to be what the compassionate 'passer-by' bade the new-born offspring of Zion to be. He was told: 'In your blood live!' Man involved in history does not live merely by the dictates of human existence but by influences coming from outside. History creates the various forms of superstructure over man. The Jew, if not affected by them, remains what he was at birth: human. The various superstructures of history transcend the human status in a radical way. Yet the commandment 'In your blood live!' means: 'be human'. With the various superstructures which are the work of creative man in history the humanity of man is changed. Exposed to the political and cultural superstructures, secular man experiences a 'second birth'.

When Paul speaks of harlotry and fornication he means harlotry and fornication. When Ezekiel and Hosea speak of harlotry and fornication, they, like all the prophets, use a metaphor. With this metaphor they face the great crisis which arose through the transition from the puritanical religion of the Fathers to the civilization of Canaan. The prophets did not agree with the orthodox Rehabites who rejected statehood, culture, civilization and temple-culture out of hand. But in one respect there was never a wavering or a going back. The Jew lives his Judaism in the family. Life in the polis, in the public sphere, was regarded as a problem which needed the utmost watchfulness, lest it might lead to an apostasy as dangerous and as despicable as harlotry and fornication. It is the apostasy in which the One and only God is forsaken for the many gods who in a highly developed civilization demand allegiance from man. Judaism must remain the faith of the 'fathers'. In biblical semantics 'fathers' does not mean a racial descent, just as the words 'in your blood live' have no racial meaning. 'Be human' is a commandment which is best fulfilled by man as a private person, in the family, but which can and should be obeyed when he leaves the private abode of his home and mixes with his fellow-men in the public, especially in the political, sector of life. The concern of the prophets was to preserve the innocent beginning, as it prevailed before the entry into history, to preserve the family spirit of kindness, warmth and equality in the midst of the diversity, inequality, competition of the political life of history. Before the entry into history, there was the fellowship of equals held together by the authority of an unchanging eternity. The prophets, and after them the rabbis, wanted to preserve this fellowship within history and deemed this possible. Paul had another cure for history: he preached brotherhood. Brotherhood binds man to man in a spiritual way. In brotherhood 'there is no such thing as Jew and Greek, slave and freeman, male and female' (Gal. 3:28).

Brotherhood is the gift of the Christian to his fellow-man. The Jew proclaims for mankind the solidarity of fellowship. Marx proclaimed the solidarity of the proletariat. He did not live to see the gentiles forsake this solidarity in 1914. Throughout the four years of World War I Lenin and Rosa Luxemburg impatiently waited for a sign of this solidarity. It did not come. The workers of Europe fought each other up to the last hour of the European fratricide. Brotherhood never prevented the Christian nations from waging war against each other.

Paul sends the runaway slave Onesimus back to his former owner. He asks for kindness towards him but to ask for his release from bondage does not occur to Paul. Brotherhood does not change inequality, fellowship does. With the understanding of the difference between fellowship and brotherhood we understand the difference between Judaism and Christianity. A recent statement of a German theologian (Joseph Ratzinger) says: 'Only somebody who is able to be a brother is able to be a Christian.' In his terminology of superstructure Marx discovered a cogent element of Christian culture. But this discovery did not make him a Christian. He did not believe in brotherhood, he believed in solidarity, in fellowship. Fellowship creates equality. Marx's belief in equality makes him a Jew.

There is a third possibility of human togetherness besides fellowship and brotherhood: friendship. The friendship between the Jew Moses Mendelssohn and the German poet Gotthold Ephraim Lessing is the first example of a new age in Europe. An intellectual bond unites the world-wide community of book-reading people, of men and women whom literature and art have made a civilized international class. Lessing, like Mendelssohn, did not want to become anybody's 'brother', but was prepared to welcome any European who was a man of letters into his friendship and communion. The friendship between Lessing and Mendelssohn initiated the century of German Jewry; the bond between German and Jew lasted up to 1933. The Zionist who rejects the creative and noble interlude of Jewish history in Germany with the indictment 'ideology of assimilation' (Rotenstreich) is blind to a happy, though certainly precarious, union of gentile and Jew. This union is neither fellowship nor brotherhood. The European book-reading community transcended national boundaries. When this union ended, it was not only the German-Jewish symbiosis which came to an end. In this union, forged by civilization, the gentile does not become a Jew nor the Jew a gentile, they approach each other in friendship. In Lessing's language friendship has no sentimental meaning. The century of the renaissance of German Jewry, which spread over Germany and reached the whole of Europe, records the history of a friendship between gentile and Jew. Judaism, whilst welcoming proselytes, is not a missionary religion. What the Jew is passionately aiming at is friendship with the gentile living near him.

We said that the commandment 'In your blood live!' refers to the always and everywhere identical *humanum*, which makes everyone, be he Jew or gentile, a creature of God. We are not concerned about alien blood but about history, a history which may or may not be compatible with the life of Jewish fellowship. It may be noble history; the Canaanites had risen to a high degree of civilization. The Israelite tribes were, in comparison with this civilization, primitive. They had to learn a lot from Canaan and they did. They also learnt things of which the prophets did not approve. They learnt to live under the code of citizenship. The fellow-citizen is no longer the neighbour of the commandment 'Love your neighbour as yourself!' Cold ethical behaviour replaced the warmth of fellowship. The fellow-man had even, under the merciless pressure of political necessity, been used as a means to an end. Somebody commanded, and others had to obey – this is the end of fellowship.

Jewish fellowship is different from the community created by the state. In Israel too, so we sincerely hope, the Jew will be more than a mere Israeli citizen. Neither common citizenship nor national status constitute Jewish fellowship. Politicians and churchmen are baffled; their categories do not apply to the social bond which binds Jew to Jew. Jewish fellowship, open to every man and every woman who wishes to enter, is closed to the press-gang which lures sons away from their fathers and sacrifices them at the altar of the state (see my analysis of the 'binding of Isaac' in Maybaum, 1969).

Gibbon in England and Nietzsche on the Continent spoke of a slave-morality which undermines the state by a bond of the weak. The weak move together, help each other, and the animal warmth of their nearness bestows intimacy on their group. Eventually the 'pariah society' succeeds in getting the better of the state. The ideology of the 'pariah society' proclaims, therefore, 'right is might', 'love wins'. The establishment of the ethics of justice and love is, it is alleged, the victory of the secret hatred with which the weak hate the strong. Nietzsche was not the first to attack the Judaeo-Christian foundation of the West with the nightmare of a pariah society. The historian Gibbon had done it before him. Gibbon summed up the six volumes of *The Decline and Fall of the Roman Empire* in the sentence: 'I have described the downfall of Rome and the rise of Christianity.' The latter was in his eyes the slave philosophy which put an end to Rome's might and glory. Various sociologists have shown Gibbon's, Nietzsche's, Wagner's and Hitler's political philosophy to be erroneous and dangerous.

It is a psychological possibility that in some cases love can be analysed and discovered as a form of hatred, and justice as a form of revenge. But a psychologically diseased man does not offer a proper example of the human mind. It can also be that the use of power is derided and even rejected in the way the fox of the fable rejects the sweet grapes as too sour for him. In this case the rejection or the criticism of the use of power is not a moral act. The psychologists – Max Scheler and his many followers – use for this the French word *ressentiment*, denoting hatred hidden in what supposes to be a moral statement or a spiritual act. The weak can be afflicted by the disease of *res-*

sentiment. Retreat into a spiritual world can, but need not, be the flight of those who cannot master life. Romans 12:20 reads: 'If your enemy is hungry, feed him, if he is thirsty, give him a drink; by doing so you will heap live coals on his head.' Here justice and love are indeed a sublime vengeance. The proclamation 'The last will be the first' needs close scrutiny. It can be the outcry of hatred which takes possession of the politically oppressed. It can be the assault with which *ressentiment* turns against the established order. In his novel *The Possessed* Dostoevsky has given us a profound psychology of man poisoned by *ressentiment*. In the Fifth Symphony Beethoven welcomes revolution as a force liberating an oppressed generation. But revolutions also set free the hatred of *ressentiment*: then bloodshed and destruction afflict the land. The hope that the weak will conquer the strong, that the few will win the battle against the many, may rise from an eschatology nourished by the hatred which the weak feel for the strong oppressor. Again, hope nourished by the fire of hatred is a disease, an affliction of the mind. But in a glorious purity of heart the Jewish worshipper proclaims in the daily service: 'And it is said, For the Lord has delivered Jacob, and redeemed him from the hand of him, that was stronger than he' (Jer. 31:11). The victory of the weak is the great miracle which sustains man on this earth.

In comparison with the enforced unity which the sovereign state displays, Jewish fellowship is a society of the weak. In comparison with a brotherhood created by a church or with the bond of 'friendship' thriving on the cultural unity of a book-reading world community, Jewish fellowship is intellectually and politically dependent on the outside world. We preserve our Jewish existence in constant assimilation to gentile culture. Jewish fellowship, not being a state or a church, always has a precarious life in history, and is often a society of persecuted and hated people. And there is indeed assimilation which can make a Jewish group disappear from the stage of history.

Jews living in the midst of gentiles will become assimilated to them. But it is foolish to turn 'assimilation' into an obscene word. In one case assimilation is to be welcomed, in another it is to be avoided. We preserve Jewish life under the constant interplay of social influences from outside. Assimilation can be a creative response to our gentile surroundings which prevents Jewish life from stagnation. We serve mankind by assimilating ourselves to gentiles: we change their aggressive mind and change our own cultural outward appearance. In this creative response of assimilation Jews do not become gentiles and gentiles do not become Jews, but a Jewish-gentile co-existence, cooperation and friendship will redeem history from being a cruel race and, every so often, from becoming a battlefield. Where Jew and gentile can live together, history becomes human.

In Jewish fellowship no king, only God, rules. 'I will not rule over you, nor shall my son; the Lord will rule over you' (Judg. 8:23). This word of Gideon is the charter of freedom given to the Jewish people. Jews must not make use of power; they must not be bosses, nor must they be obedient sheep. Abstention from the use of power makes Jews Jews, and in this they represent mankind, because the vast majority of mankind has no power and all men yearn for a situation in which power will not compel anyone: the wolf and the lamb will dwell together. This attitude to power makes the Jew different from the gentiles, different from both ruler and ruled and makes him the 'Paraclete', the Servant of God in his vicarious suffering, as the Book of the Second Isaiah describes him. *Ecce homo!* Look at the Jew, he is man, truly man. As man he is the Paraclete, that is to say the advocate of man before God. And he is also the comforter of man, bringing the good tidings that the human situation is not one of despair. Look at the Jew: he lives among the gentiles and is alive. Nobody can pass him without marvelling at a fact which is unbelievable and yet true: the Jew exists in his weakness and is not swallowed up by the mighty. Advocate, intercessor and comforter, these attributes of the Paraclete (John 14:16, 26, etc.) belong to the Jew of the diaspora in and outside the State of Israel.

Jews confess their status in the words: 'Blessed art Thou, O Lord, who hast chosen us from all peoples.' Viewed with the eyes of the gentiles, the Jewish people is a group of outcasts and aliens. The election of the Jewish people is not seen. That

M

those who bless the Jewish people will themselves be blessed, is one point. That those who curse the Jewish people will themselves be cursed, is the other. The people chosen to dissolve the national separation of the gentiles into a united mankind is seen as a curse by those who desire to remain gentiles. The gentiles, in the glory of their states, churches, cultures, are the nobility of the present day, and they regard those outside their clans as pariah-people. A pariah-people is not an empirical nation. To speak of a pariah-people is to apply a term of abuse. This abuse eventually creates an empirical group. In this way the anti-Semite forges a social reality out of what is only a figment of his hateful imagination.

Jesus said to the rabbis: 'Do not presume to say to yourselves, "We have Abraham for our father". I tell you that God can make children for Abraham out of these stones here' (Matt. 3:9). Jesus and the rabbis are concerned with different issues. Jesus rejects a racial understanding of Jewish existence. Jews have always done this. But the rabbis in their opposition to the assumed word of Jesus reject a spiritualization of Jewish existence. Jewish existence can be transformed into, and expressed by, a set of doctrines. The result of this transformation is a Second Israel, an Israel in the spirit, an Israel conceived in the conversion of the Israel of the flesh into the Israel of the spirit. A conversion into a spiritual Israel is not a Jewish proposition. It would mean a conversion of the people into a church. The rabbis contradict Jesus with their faithfulness to a physical Israel. Christianity is conversion into the Israel of the spirit, the transformation of a people into a spiritual institution, into a church. The rabbis do and must reject this. They reject the very experience of conversion. It is a Christian experience. 'Out of stones', Jesus said, children can issue to Abraham. Such is the view of a faith soaring to spiritual height. This view explains the difference between the Jewish people and the Christian Church. The Church is an Israel in the spirit, Israel is a people in the flesh. The Jew obeys the commandment 'In thy blood live!' When the Jew makes *kiddush*, he blesses the bread and eats this precious gift of God, and he drinks the wine from the cup, whereas the Christian performs the ritual of the Holy Communion. The Jew understands what is meant by the word 'spiritual'; the Christian as disciple of the Jew understands, of course, the distinction between holy and profane. But the Jew constitutes his Judaism, lives his Jewish life, with the distinction holy and profane; the Christian constitutes his life by understanding and applying the distinction between spiritual and secular. Antiquity did not know of a secular life. The Christian faith created it. The profane world, on the other hand, is not like the secular world. The profane world is life outside the holy realm (*pro-fanum*) but remains unchanged.

The Dutch theologian Arend T. van Leeuwen calls secular civilization 'Christianity incognito'. Creative man is the architect of Western civilization. The West sees creative man driven by God. The Western belief is challenged by Islam. Islam means submission. In submission to God man is able to pray. The spirit which fills the heart of the worshipper and the spirit which drives creative man have to be acknowledged as different, although the Jew will say: in God the two are one.

Islam treats Western civilization with suspicion, because it sees Christianity as a danger to Islam. The late Lord Cromer has expressed what the vast majority of Muslim theologians teach: Islam reformed is no longer Islam. The Jew has to make a decision between the contrasting views of Christianity and Islam. A doctrinal formula is not forthcoming here. Through his prophetic Judaism the Jew will do justice to Islam and Christianity; both have their origin in Judaism. But the Jew guided by prophetic Judaism will go his own way, which is neither the way of the Christian nor that of the Muslim. Both Christianity and Islam will profit from the Jewish form of monotheism which pursues the aims of Western civilization but does not identify itself with it.

CHAPTER IV

Summary

'We walk with God and without religion.' This statement of Rosenzweig, which I quoted on p. 81, loses its provocative character when we understand it in the way in which the term 'prophetic Judaism' is understood by Abraham Geiger and by the great majority of the German rabbis. Christianity and Islam are established religions; Paul and Mohammed are the founders of their respective monotheistic religions. Judaism, always close to the biblical prophets, need not become an established religion.

Judaism gave birth to Christianity and to Islam, and so the Jew both accepts and rejects some principles and some parts of Christianity and Islam. It is not always appropriate to see Judaism as different from Christianity and Islam. Judaism is not always different from, it is also sometimes identical with these two religions. The prophetic independence of the Jew can sometimes hail the two established forms of monotheism, Christianity and Islam, with the warm sympathy in which a kinsman, a real brother, is embraced. But firm opposition, from which Jews cannot go back an inch in their encounter with Christianity and Islam, is also equally necessary. This double task makes Judaism rather a prophetic movement than an established religion.

In his encounter with Christianity Rosenzweig shows no interest in the historian's endeavour to recover the historical Jesus. The historian will only find in the past what he sees in the present.

The liberal historian will discover Jesus the Reformer. The historian who is a socialist will find Jesus the champion of the poor. The Zionist will be in sympathy with Jesus the hero of a Jewish nationalist rising against Rome. There have been as many types of the historical Jesus in the nineteenth and twentieth centuries as the ideologies that these centuries have brought forth. The latest form in which Jesus has been presented to us is *Jesus Christ Superstar*.

Rosenzweig regarded the discovery of the historical Jesus as an illusion. But even if historical research, which must go on, should one day be successful and find the historical Jesus, against Rosenzweig's expectation, this discovery would not have any impact on the understanding of Christianity. Rosenzweig, most eager to understand the difference between Judaism and Christianity, turned to the Jesus of the Christian Church, to the Jesus of the Christian faith.

There is the word 'spiritual'. What does it mean? The Christian knows the answer, the Muslim does not. He rejects the dichotomy between matter and spirit, between body and soul, between secular and spiritual. When the Jew regards what the Christian calls spirit as the spirit of man, this Jewish acknowledgment is blasphemy in the eyes of the Christian. The Jew, who has moved away from Islamic surroundings and in the West has come near to Christian culture, will not, as does the Muslim, recoil from the realm called 'spiritual' by the Christian. Yet Franz Rosenzweig radically repudiated Christianity, saying '(The Jewish people) does not have to hire the services of the spirit' (*Star*, p. 299 and pp. 157–67 of this book). Here Rosenzweig, although lovingly disposed towards Christianity, is on the side of Islam. Here we see the double task of prophetic encounter, both affirming and rejecting, in Rosenzweig's attitude to Christianity. Here he is of the same opinion as his teacher Hermann Cohen, who said: 'Jesus Christ – a god! Never has anybody really believed this' (see p. 155). Of course Rosenzweig is more erudite in Christian theology than Cohen; he knows the conjectures of the doctrine of the Trinity and knows that Christianity is in spite of its faith in Christ a monotheistic religion. But his understanding of the spirit makes Rosenzweig as radical as Cohen. He would not speak of spiritual Judaism as did the anti-Zionists in their fight against political Judaism. Spiritual Judaism exists: the Christian Church is spiritual Judaism. The doctrine of universalism and the doctrinal attribute 'spiritual' are household words of the nineteenth-century anti-Zionist. Anti-Zionist universalism is Christian universalism. The Church is a universal Church. The universalism of the biblical prophets was connected with the contingencies of the place and the time of their mission.

The state, like the Christian Church, uproots man from tribe and family and thus creates the spiritual situation characteristic of man as citizen and as soldier. 'The services of the spirit' are 'hired' to shape man for the *polis*. The state, just like the Church, changes man formed by the tribe and the family into 'another man', capable of being a citizen and a soldier. The state is the holder and user of power, not only in war but also in peace. The emancipation of *jus* from *rus*, the transformation of the husband-man into man obeying a man-made law (see p. 95) is a process effected by force. It is a process entailing tragedy and suffering. The Jew can hail the Jewish State as a precious gift granted to him. He can be a citizen and can be a soldier after the fashion of Greek antiquity. Yet the Jew must not become reduced to what citizens and soldiers are. They are lifted to the tragic realm of the spirit which constitutes both State and Church. Prophetic Judaism's double task of affirmation and negation presents itself here. We must say 'yes', and we must know when to say 'no'. A politicized and spiritualized Judaism – Jews entirely and exclusively characterized as citizens and soldiers – is not the Judaism to which prophetic Judaism aspires.

The same critical attitude of agreement and disagreement which we observe towards Christianity has to be applied towards Islam. In the *Kulturkampf*, which has already started in Israel and which will and must go on, there are, as mentioned before, rabbis who are rightly called *ulema*-rabbis, orthodox rabbis who defend their form of Judaism with Islamic doctrines. 'The gate of *ijtihad* has been closed' is the stock answer to would-be reformers: any interpretation which leads away from the *sunna* (the beaten path) is excluded. The rabbinic doctrine of oral law, which has always made a progressive interpretation of Judaism possible, has no equivalent in orthodox Islam. Both Islamic divines and orthodox rabbis, when approached for help against a petrified law, turn to their doctrine which does not allow any change. (In fact there are already Islamic scholars who have the courage to initiate a modern progressive Islam.) *Ijma* guards against encroachment through any interpretation originating in the conviction of the personal conscience. 'Islam is what the Muslim believes it to be.' 'My congregation will never fall victim to error', taught Mohammed. Islam must not be exposed to historical criticism but must remain based on the consensus of the members of the established order. Prophetic Judaism must battle against Islam which influences Judaism with an attempted and all too often successful 'fixation', as Western scholars of Islam call it. Fixation must not be defended as conservatism, it is the oriental feature of Levantine civilization. The constant interplay of both progress and conservatism is the hallmark of European civilization.

We come now to the most dangerous infiltration of Islamic thought to be seen in the transformation of the concept of the Torah into a myth. The Koran is scripture 'for the unscriptured', it is a book which does not reveal its entire holiness when approached with the intellect. The 'unscriptured' revere the Koran as an awe-inspiring miracle, as a *mysterium tremendum et fascinosum*. The Torah of the orthodox rabbis has the same character. The Torah with which the orthodox group are equipped for the battle against the progressives has become a Jewish Koran. The Torah which has made the Jewish people a most intellectual group has become a myth. A myth does not educate, does not adduce arguments, does not appeal to the personal conscience, a myth is a banner leading men in orgiastic drunkenness into battle. The Torah as a myth transforms Judaism into Islam, a form of Islam without Islam's piety.

There are the texts in Isaiah concerning the Suffering Servant and his mission to be a 'light to the nations'. These texts have been forged into an anti-Zionist ideology. Emil Fackenheim, one of the few theologians left in post-holocaust Jewry, agrees with the

Islamic rejection of the role of suffering. 'We have suffered enough', he says. Here our double task of agreement and disagreement confronts the Jew with both Christianity and Islam. Our answer can be neither the Christian answer nor that of the Muslim. The patriarchs are honoured figures in the Koran, whereas the prophets from the eighth century B.C.E. onwards are entirely absent. The sequence stops with Elijah and Elisha. The Koran does not include Amos, Hosea, the Isaiahs or Jeremiah. The prophets who accept suffering as a vocation in the process of redemption have no place in Islam with its sense of history as manifest success. Which figure represents history: the crucified prophet or Mohammed, the victorious prophet? Is the Christian or the Muslim view of history right? Should Jewish preachers remind Jews again and again of the six million martyrs who perished in the holocaust? Or should they urge their flock to rejoice in the establishment of the State of Israel? The decision to preach either the one sermon or the other, or a combination of both, is the one laid upon the shoulders of a preacher challenged to speak neither like a Christian nor like a Muslim but like a biblical prophet. Nobody can tell him what to say. His sermon may be a fitting part of a Bar Mitsvah service, which unites relatives, young and old, as a happy crowd in festive clothes, expressing the historic fact: Hitler has not won, 'we are here, we have survived' (Fackenheim, 1970). Or his sermon may contradict the happiness of the worshippers with his constant sombre reminder that man has to carry the heavy yoke of a mission.

Finally, there is the Islamic tenet of *Tauhid*, 'the effective assertion of God to end the gods'. Islam can enter into Jewish orthodoxy, especially in a *Kulturkampf*, and infect it with iconoclasm. But Zechariah's 'The Lord is One and His name One' (14:9) is not the Muslim's: 'There is no god but God.' The Muslim deprives the idols of the right to be worshipped, but they are for him realities which have to be fought against passionately. This fanatical confession, inciting to holy wars, is not in the words of Zechariah. To him the idols are *elilim*, nothings. You can safely ignore them. God will deal with them. This prophetic understanding of the unity calms man's heart not with neutrality, but with the peace of mind which regards the victory of God as certain and as in no need of the assistance of political force and power. But the Islamic tenet of *Tauhid*, 'There is no god but God', associates itself with the political forces of history. It is entirely different with the biblical prophet. His *Adonai echad*, the 'God is One' of the 'Hear, O Israel', expresses the unity of heart in which all illusions, fears, ambitions and superstitions die out in a single committal.

With this difference between the Jewish *Yichud* and the Islamic *Tauhid* in mind, we make the first step towards overcoming the division between Jews confessing the 'Hear, O Israel' and Jews singing the *Hatikvah*, the Jewish national anthem. But a second step is still necessary. We must overcome not only Islamic, but also Christian influence.

A national anthem has a deep religious content. Think of the 'Marseillaise', or of any national anthem of Western post-medieval men. In a national anthem man turns to God, but not to God 'and nothing besides Him'. There is something besides Him. Philo called it *Logos*, we may call it history, embracing state, culture and other creations of man; the Christian will speak of a mediator. Here is the point where Jews may become like the Christian gentiles, worshipping God and something besides Him, changing biblical monotheism, Jewish monotheism, into Christian monotheism. Jews of the Zionist era accept state, homeland and culture as substitutes for religion. Western rabbis of the nineteenth century spoke of dry baptism, of Jews who do not become baptized, shrink back from the very idea of becoming baptized, but move towards baptism by the force of history. With the 'Hear, O Israel, God is One', state, homeland, indeed the whole of history, are robbed of their faculty of becoming religious absolutes. With the 'Hear, O Israel' alive in their hearts Jews will easily overcome not merely the clash between the *Hatikvah* and 'God save the Queen', but also and above all the clash between the Oneness of God and everything history has to offer. The citizens of the Jewish State and the soldiers defending it express in their national anthem their loyalty to the state and their fellow-citizens. With their 'Hear, O Israel, God is One' Israelis remain Jews and do not become Israeli gentiles.

The Jewish diaspora has all the characteristics of an international society. In coining the phrase 'blood and soil' Fascism has given us a new definition of pagan man: man rooted in the soil. The Jew of the diaspora is the opposite of this type of man. The 'soil' of world history is exhausted. The rise of a type of man capable of existing when uprooted from the soil promises to be of great help. Diaspora Jews, uprooted from the soil for two millennia, follow in the footsteps of those who have built centres of civilization. Jews have their habitat where the state does its civilizing work. The State of Israel is greatly helped in its contribution to civilization by its closeness to the diaspora. When we call the diaspora *galut*, this Hebrew connotation reminds us that both the State of Israel and the diaspora outside Israel are *galut*: as long as the Messiah has not yet come, every community lives in the *galut*, in the unredeemed history of man chosen to carry the yoke of the *galut*, moving in travail, in suffering and in hope towards the kingdom of God.

Bibliography

Baeck, Leo (1948), *The Essence of Judaism*, Schocken
Buber, M. (1927), *Die chassidischen Bücher*, Schocken
Buber, M. (1948), *Israel and the World: Essays in a Time of Crisis*, Schocken
Buber, M. (1949), *Paths in Utopia*, Routledge & Kegan Paul
Buber, M. (1952), *Israel and Palestine: The History of an Idea*, East and West
  Library, London; Farrar, Strauss & Young, New York
Buber, M. (1953), *Eclipse of God*, Gollancz
Bullock, A. (1970), 'Europe since Hitler', *International Affairs*, vol. 47, no. 1,
  November
Casper, Bernhard (1967), *Das dialogische Denken*, Herder, Freiburg
Cassirer, Ernst (1929), 'Die Idee der Religion', in *Festgabe zum zehnjährigen
  Bestehen der Akademie fuer die Wissenschaft des Judentums*, Berlin
Cragg, G. R. (1962), *The Church and the Age of Reason*, Hodder
Cragg, K. (1965), *The Call of the Minaret*, Oxford University Press (Galaxy
  books)
Cragg, K. (1970), *Alive to God: Muslim and Christian Prayer*, Oxford University
  Press
Cutler, A. (1968), 'The origins of modern anti-Semitism: a new hypothesis',
  Judaism, Autumn, vol. 17, no. 4
Fackenheim, E. L. (1970), *God's Presence in History*, London University Press
Geiger, L. (1910), *Abraham Geiger, Leben und Lebenswerk*, Berlin
Gibb, H. A. R. and Kramers, J. H. (eds) (1953), *Shorter Encyclopaedia of Islam*,
  Brill, Leiden
Glatzer, Nahum (1953), *Franz Rosenzweig: His Life and Thought*, Schocken.
  'The New Thinking' and 'The True and the False Messiah' are two chapters
  in this book, the first being a translation of passages from *Das neue Denken*,
  originally published in German in Rosenzweig's *Kleinere Schriften* (see
  Rosenzweig, E. 1937); the second is a translation from Rosenzweig's com-
  mentary to *Jehuda Halevi*
Goddard, Harold C. (1969) in J. Wilders (ed.), *The Merchant of Venice: A
  Collection of Critical Essays*, Macmillan (Casebook series)

Guardini, Romano (1922), *Ecclesia Orans I*, Freiburg

Heppe, H. (1879), *Geschichte des Pietismus, . . . in der reformierten Kirche namentlich der Niederlande*

Hertz, J. H. (ed.) (1947), *The Authorised Daily Prayer Book of the United Hebrew Congregation of the British Empire*, Shapiro, Vallentine

Hodgson, Leonard (1968), *For Faith and Freedom: Gifford Lectures, 1955–7*, S.C.M.P.

Huizinga, J. (1924), *The Waning of the Middle Ages*, Arnold

Huizinga, J. (1960), 'In Commemoration of Erasmus' in *Men and Ideas*, Eyre & Spottiswoode

Huizinga, J. (1970), *Homo Ludens: A Study of the Play Element in Culture*, Temple Smith

Kaufmann, Walter (1970), *I and Thou*, Scribner

Klausner, J. (1922), *Jesus of Nazareth*, trans. H. Danby, Allen & Unwin

Kohn, Hans (1961), *Martin Buber, His Life and Times*, Melzer, Cologne

Landauer, G. (1920), *Shakespeare*, Rütten & Löning, Frankfurt

Laqueur, W. (1970), *Europe Since Hitler*, Weidenfeld & Nicolson

Maybaum, I. (1960), *Jewish Existence*, Vallentine, Mitchell

Maybaum, I. (1969), *Creation and Guilt*, Vallentine, Mitchell

Ortega y Gasset, José (1951), *The Revolt of the Masses*, Allen & Unwin

Ortega y Gasset, José (1967), *On Love: Aspects of a Single Theme*, trans. T. Talbot, Cape

Rosenstock, Eugen (1969), *Judaism Despite Christianity*, University of Alabama Press

Rosenzweig, Edith (ed.) (1937), *Kleinere Schriften*, Schocken/Jüdischer Buchverlag, Berlin

Rosenzweig, Edith and Simon, Ernst (eds) (1935), *Briefe*, Berlin

Rosenzweig, F. (1924), *The Builders* (pamphlet) in M. Buber (ed.), *Der Jude*, vol. 8. Later published in *Kleinere Schriften* (see Rosenzweig, E., 1937)

Rosenzweig, F. (1927), *Jehuda Halevi*, Lambert Schneider, Berlin

Rosenzweig, F. (1971), *The Star of Redemption*, trans. W. W. Hallo, Routledge & Kegan Paul

Safrai, S. (1965), 'Teaching of Pietists in Mishnaic Literature', *Journal of Jewish Studies*, vol. 16, nos 1–2

Sandmel, S. (1965) *We Jews and Jesus*, Gollancz

Steiner, G. (1967), *Language and Silence: Essays and Notes, 1958–66*, Faber

Steiner, G. (1971), *In Bluebeard's Castle*, Faber. First published in the *Listener*, April 1971, p. 446

Stern, G. (1934), *Der Weg ohne Ende*, Berlin

Tawney, R. H. (1925), 'Introduction' to Thomas Wilson, *A Discourse upon Usury*, Bell

Weiss, J. G. (1957), 'A circle of pre-Hasidic pneumatics', *Journal of Jewish Studies*, vol. 8

Weltsch, R. (ed.) (1961), *Leo Baeck Year-Book*, East and West Library, London, Jerusalem, New York

Wilders, J. (ed.) (1969), *Shakespeare, 'The Merchant of Venice'*, Macmillan

Index